Designing API-First Enterprise Architectures on Azure

A guide for architects and developers to expedite digital transformation with API-led architectures

Subhajit Chatterjee

BIRMINGHAM—MUMBAI

Designing API-First Enterprise Architectures on Azure

Copyright © 2021 Packt Publishing

Group Product Manager: Richa Tripathi

Publishing Product Manager: Kushal Dave

Senior Editor: Ruvika Rao

Content Development Editors: Ananya Endow, Kinnari Chohan

Technical Editor: Pradeep Sahu

Copy Editor: Safis Editing

Project Coordinator: Ajesh Devavaram

Proofreader: Safis Editing

Indexer: Subalakshmi Govindhan

Production Designer: Alishon Mendonca

First Published: July 2021

Production reference: 1160721

Published by Packt Publishing Ltd.
Livery Place
35 Livery Street
Birmingham
B3 2PB, UK.

ISBN 978-1-80181-391-4

www.packt.com

To my mother, Krishna Chatterjee, and my father, the late Nirmalendu Chatterjee, whose countless sacrifices have made me the man that I am today.

To my elder brother, Abhijit, without whose support and guidance I wouldn't have come this far.

To my loving wife, Tamanna, for believing in me and keeping me motivated.

To my daughter, Tanusha, who makes me a proud father.

– Subhajit Chatterjee

Contributors

About the author

Subhajit Chatterjee completed his bachelor's degree in engineering from NITK, Surathkal, India, way back in 2002. He also holds a postgraduate diploma in information technology from Amity University. Aside from this, he has undertaken various other online certifications that have helped him to learn and grow as a software engineering professional.

Subhajit has close to two decades of exposure to designing, implementing, and managing software development projects, using Microsoft and open source technologies. He currently works as a solutions architect with Microsoft Consulting Services, leading large and complex projects in Azure, IoT, enterprise integrations, web applications, and mobility space.

Subhajit loves to solve problems and has had the privilege of working with customers across the globe. He is passionate about sharing what he learns with the community. He believes in continuous learning and enjoys coaching and mentoring others for professional enrichment.

I wish to thank the people who have been close to me and supported me, especially all my colleagues and mentors who have shared their knowledge and experiential learning with me.

About the reviewer

Niloshima Srivastava has around 12 years of experience working as Software Architect in a Product Based Organization. She is a graduate in CSE and holds several Cloud Certifications on Azure/AWS. She has been an evangelist when it comes to Microsoft platforms, augmented by being a hands-on developer, solution architect, and outstanding illustrator of design concepts and methodology. Not the least but proven track records even in training and orchestrating what she has learned to new rising developers across various platforms on various forums.

Table of Contents

Section 2: Build Reliable API-Centric Solutions

3
Architecture Principles and API Styles

4

Assuring the Quality of the API Service (or Product)

5
RESTful APIs – the New Web

6
API Design Practices

Section 3: Deliver Business Value for a Modern Enterprise

8
API-Centric Enterprise Integrations

9

APIs as a Monetized Product

Other Books You May Enjoy

Index

Preface

Rapid adoption of cloud technologies has revolutionized the way modern-day applications are architected and implemented. Solution architects and IT decision-makers are constantly faced with the challenge to quickly adapt to the latest technology trends to establish a competitive advantage in the marketplace. Gartner has predicted that by 2025, about 80% of enterprises will have shifted their operations to the cloud. Hence, it has become even more imperative that enterprises pay attention to their digital transformation roadmaps to benefit from their cloud-first and mobile-first initiatives. Tactically, this means a lot of changes on the ground, including reinventing business processes, adopting agile and DevOps best practices, and even embarking on the modernization of operations.

API-led architecture is not something new – rather, it has just become a lot more relevant and important in today's world. Cloud computing offers three key benefits: flexibility, efficiency, and strategic value. API-led connectivity has changed the way enterprises interact with their customers and partners. Customers today are very demanding. They expect businesses to be agile and adapt to their demands. They prefer a simple and intuitive approach to meeting their needs. They are open to the use of technology and apps to get the job done in just a few steps. Thus, enterprises are required to utilize the insights derived from analyzing customer behavior as the basis for their digital innovation strategies.

Over the past few years, I have worked with multiple enterprise customers to define their blueprints for a robust and reliable API-led solution. However, the common challenge has been in getting them to understand the benefits of this approach, as it requires some initial investment and work prioritization. It was always a hard sell unless the key stakeholders had prior experience with implementing solutions using a **service-oriented architecture** (**SOA**) approach. Many lacked the appetite to incur any additional complexity on top of what they were used to. It was also a revelation to me that teams weren't too well versed in the concept of microservices. Everybody wanted to do it, but nobody seemed to know how to approach it. A few believed that splitting a large monolith into smaller services was, in effect, building microservices. While this was still a good starting point, it lacked a futuristic vision, as the many other aspects of a microservices architecture were not considered as part of the design process. The technical teams were also getting used to the new way of building solutions and would often miss out on the fundamentals, leading to problems later in the life cycle. Teams often lacked a production-first mindset as many of the important architecture-critical requirements were deferred to later.

In this book, it has been my endeavor to provide a glimpse of the "whole nine yards" that is essential for the successful delivery of an API-led enterprise solution. This book focuses on the latest emerging trends in the industry, supplementing theoretical concepts with real-world scenarios and examples to help you grasp the concepts more easily. The book touches upon the important principles and practices that can eventually serve as a checklist for development teams. While I have used the Microsoft Azure cloud as the platform of choice, the topics discussed are valid even for a multi-cloud scenario as well.

After reading this book, you will be well versed in how to architect, design, implement, deploy, and maintain a digital service.

Who this book is for

This book is meant to serve as a ready reckoner for solution architects, developers, and IT and business decision-makers as they are taken through a journey showing how to approach their API-led connectivity requirements. The book has been written from a practitioner's point of view, with lots of tips, practical guidance, and additional references that will surely provide clarity of thought for developers, allowing them to confidently prepare for their next API-first architecture implementation.

What this book covers

Chapter 1, Evolution of Enterprise Solution Architectures, gives you a background on the evolution of enterprise architectures, from SOA to a more microservices-based approach, and discusses how the adoption of open standards will help advance the building of interconnected experiences in the evolution process.

Chapter 2, APIs as Digital Connectors, walks you through the concept of a connected enterprise, emphasizing the role and importance of APIs in fueling the growth of the digital economy.

Chapter 3, Architecture Principles and API Styles, provides an overview of important architecture principles that are the basis for the foundation of any API platform. The chapter also covers the popular architecture styles that are frequently used in an enterprise and how they can be implemented in the Azure cloud.

Chapter 4, Assuring the Quality of the API Service (or Product), focuses on the quality attributes that are critical for the success of API solutions. It also explains how to make use of the Azure Well-Architected Framework to design, implement, and measure the quality of service for your API solutions.

Chapter 5, RESTful APIs – The New Web Standard, covers some of the best practices that must be followed while designing and implementing RESTful-style API interfaces, which are becoming a new web standard.

Chapter 6, API Design Practices, discusses the important design practices that must be followed while building your API-centric solutions. It also briefly covers the different patterns that are commonly used for implementing your API microservices.

Chapter 7, Accelerating through DevOps Essentials, focuses on the essential DevOps practices that must be followed by the engineering teams to drive greater IT maturity across the broad spectrum of the enterprise.

Chapter 8, API-Centric Enterprise Integrations, takes a deeper look into some real-world enterprise integration scenarios and considers how the Azure Integration Services offering can be utilized for this purpose.

Chapter 9, API as a Monetized Product, discusses how enterprises can realize greater business value and improve their revenue streams by applying an intelligent productization strategy for their API assets.

To get the most out of this book

This book is intended for audiences who are likely to have a role in either defining and/or implementing API-centric solutions. Hence, it is recommended that you apply the inferences shared to your own practical requirements and do further self-study and analysis to better understand the concepts presented.

Download the color images

We also provide a PDF file that has color images of the screenshots/diagrams used in this book. You can download it here: `https://static.packt-cdn.com/downloads/9781801813914_ColorImages.pdf`.

Conventions used

There are a number of text conventions used throughout this book.

`Code in text`: Indicates code words in text, database table names, folder names, filenames, file extensions, pathnames, dummy URLs, user input, and Twitter handles. Here is an example: "For example, say the URI `/api/policies/id` returned the policy resource for the specified ID. Then the URL `/api/policies/id/assets` will return all the assets linked to the respective policy."

A block of code is set as follows:

```
GET /policy/getPolicy?id=POLICY1122334455 HTTP/1.1
Host: api.contoso.inc
```

When we wish to draw your attention to a particular part of a code block, the relevant lines or items are set in bold:

```
https://api.packinsurance.com/quotingservice/getquote?api-version=1.0
```

```
https://api.packinsurance.com/quotingservice/getquote?api-version=2.0
```

Bold: Indicates a new term, an important word, or words that you see on screen. For example, words in menus or dialog boxes appear in the text like this. Here is an example: "Observe that **Quote Service (Basic)** is accessible to **Guests**."

> **Tips or important notes**
> Appear like this.

Get in touch

Feedback from our readers is always welcome.

General feedback: If you have questions about any aspect of this book, mention the book title in the subject of your message and email us at customercare@packtpub.com.

Errata: Although we have taken every care to ensure the accuracy of our content, mistakes do happen. If you have found a mistake in this book, we would be grateful if you would report this to us. Please visit www.packtpub.com/support/errata, selecting your book, clicking on the Errata Submission Form link, and entering the details.

Piracy: If you come across any illegal copies of our works in any form on the internet, we would be grateful if you would provide us with the location address or website name. Please contact us at copyright@packt.com with a link to the material.

If you are interested in becoming an author: If there is a topic that you have expertise in, and you are interested in either writing or contributing to a book, please visit authors.packtpub.com.

Share Your Thoughts

Once you've read *Designing API-First Enterprise Architectures on Azure*, we'd love to hear your thoughts! Scan the QR code below to go straight to the Amazon review page for this book and share your feedback.

https://packt.link/r/1801813914

Your review is important to us and the tech community and will help us make sure we're delivering excellent quality content.

Section 1: API-Led Architecture in the Digital Economy

In the first part of the book, you will discover why API-based integration architectures within enterprises are increasing, and how they are beneficial compared to traditional approaches to expedite digital transformation in a cloud-first, mobile-first world.

This section includes the following chapters:

- *Chapter 1, Evolution of Enterprise Solution Architectures*
- *Chapter 2, APIs as Digital Connectors*

1
Evolution of Enterprise Solution Architectures

An **enterprise application** is a large software system platform, typically comprising multiple applications that are designed to assist the organization in solving its business problems in a well-coordinated fashion. These platforms are complex, generally evolve over a period, and must be scalable and extensible. They are largely driven by the strategic technology initiatives that are identified to accomplish the vision and business objectives of the organization.

The purpose of this chapter is to share insights on how enterprise solution architectures have evolved from being a collection of standalone monoliths to **service-oriented architectures** (**SOA**) to a more modern microservices-based solution approach in recent times.

Over the past decade, there has been a significant rise in the demand for omnichannel and interconnected experiences. Be it the consumerization of IT or mobile-first applications, emergingtechnology trends have created a compelling need for businesses to invest in **cloud-native applications (CNCF)** or integrate with **Software-as-a-Service (SaaS)** product offerings. If you are new to these terms, a brief explanation follows:

- CNCF: Cloud-native applications are typically modern applications designed to run on the cloud using the recommended cloud architecture and design principles. They are mostly microservices hosted using managed services to offer great scale and performance.

- SaaS: Software as a Service refers to the model of hosting a software solution or product on the cloud. This is accessible over the internet using a subscription or pay-as-you-go model.

> **Note**
> You can make use of the links provided in the *Further reading* section to understand the preceding concepts in greater detail.

In this chapter, we are going to cover the following main topics:

- History of application architectures in an enterprise

- IT strategies in the modern world

- The emergence of API-led architectures

    By the end of this chapter, you will understand how to prioritize your IT solutions strategy for any upcoming digital transformation projects.

> **Disclaimer**
> The topics presented in this chapter assume that you have a basic level of understanding of solution architectures in an enterprise context. At the end of the chapter, additional suggested reading links have been provided for you to review and explore more on the various topics.

History of application architectures in an enterprise

A solution architecture is typically the outcome of the bundle of ideas and experiences that you may apply to any specific business and customer context in order to meet a specific vision, within the constraints of timelines and budget availability.

Over the past two to three decades, organizations have progressively invested in building enterprise applications and systems that aim to do the following:

- Provide a competitive advantage.
- Reduce wastage and manual effort.
- Limit costs to improve revenue and profit.

The primary goals have always revolved around a few key priorities, such as improving business processes for greater productivity, timely decision-making ability, and the seamless flow of information across various siloed systems and channels to foster more effective coordination among various departments and personnel within the enterprise.

From monoliths to SOA and microservices

With the evolution of the World Wide Web around early 2000, the adoption of IT within enterprises gained momentum. Information was accessible remotely, thereby opening up new avenues of business collaboration:

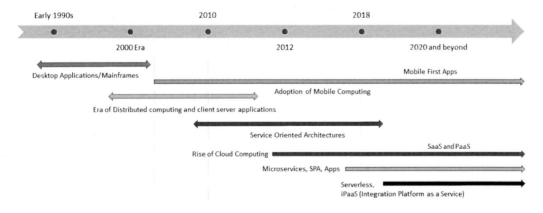

Figure 1.1 – Solution architecture trends

Since early 2010, enterprises have started leaning toward mobile apps as their primary channel to offer an online experience to their customers. Over the past decade, there have been tremendous advances in the field of mobile technology, especially with internet connectivity and mobile devices being a viable alternative to desktop computing devices. This has led to a surge in the present-day user-friendly business apps, enabling users to get a job done from anywhere in just a few steps.

Furthermore, the evolution of cloud computing technologies has revolutionized how enterprises plan to deploy their **line-of-business** (**LOB**) applications. CNCF and online services (SaaS) served as game-changers for enterprises. The cloud offered the promise of elastic scale, with high performance and availability. This was possible through managed services and scaling on-demand capabilities available on all public clouds. Basically, the cloud provider would manage the underlying server infrastructure to meet the workload demands. This allowed enterprises to modernize their business and work environments.

There was a gradual decline in the traditional development style of building applications, leading to a more microservices-based approach. By making use of this approach, complex and massive distributed systems can easily be broken down into smaller components, also termed **microservices**.

Microservices are self-contained and can be independently deployed and scaled. These microservices perform just one business function and are relatively easy to change and upgrade without impacting the broader ecosystem of services. This approach allows enterprises to take a more customer-centric approach and react quickly to market demands. The differences between microservices and monoliths are explained later in this chapter.

As was evident in the years that followed, *Solution Architecture Blueprints* progressively shifted from monoliths to microservices-based architectures, preferably deployed in the cloud. With these changing trends, developers shifted their focus to building robust API platforms comprising granular and loosely coupled microservices, with each service acting as a business sub-system serving a specific purpose within the ecosystem. These API platforms can be easily integrated with, and consumed from, lightweight mobile or web apps.

For your understanding, the following are the differences between microservices, mini-services, and monoliths (or macroservices):

- **Microservice**: This refers to a granular unit of a business functionality that can be independently developed, deployed (as a service), and managed without having a significant dependency on other services around it. It is loosely coupled and is based on the single-responsibility principle.

- **Mini-service**: This refers to a group or collection of microservices that come together as a unit to solve a specific business functionality. Typically, this group of microservices is deployed on a common infrastructure and shares any underlying database.

- **Monolith** or **macroservice**: This refers to the legacy way of building applications, wherein all business services were deployed as a single package on an application server. The components in the system were tightly coupled and have less complexity in both design and deployment. System upgrades were expensive, even requiring downtime.

> **Note**
> Refer to the following article to understand more about the differences:
> `https://thenewstack.io/miniservices-a-realistic-alternative-to-microservices/.`

IT strategies in the modern world

The unprecedented disruption to economies as a result of the COVID-19 pandemic has forced CTOs to rethink and reinvent their IT strategies and roadmaps. It was obvious that companies had to expedite their digital transformation journeys to stay in business, or else they risked losing out to their competitors.

The constantly evolving digital ecosystem is driving companies to reimagine their relationships with their customers, suppliers, and employees by engaging in ways that were not possible before.

Let's explore the motivating forces driving digital transformation initiatives.

Outlook for digital transformation

As per Gartner, for success in this new era, the corporate vision for all enterprises must shift toward *business outcome-driven strategies*. The consumerization of IT has led to the enormous growth and adoption of mobile and cloud technologies, both of which are now considered critical enablers for digital transformations:

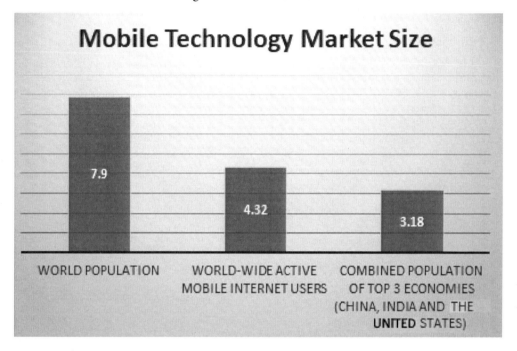

Figure 1.2 – Mobile technology market size as of March 31, 2021

In this rapidly changing competitive landscape, companies that demonstrate greater adaptability are able to survive through the disruption in the industry as different business models are constantly evolving, along with different ways to deliver a service.

However, it must also be noted that digital transformation is not easily achievable. Business and IT leaders must strive to remove the boundaries of corporate silos and innovate in terms of their IT roadmaps to create more inclusive and interconnected digital experiences for their customers, partners, and employees.

In summary, to address the compelling demands of the market and to establish a truly distinct and differentiated offering, enterprises must propel their digital transformation agendas toward the following:

- Adopting an API-first architecture to support resilient operations
- Decoupling frontend presentation from backend data functionality

- Capturing and visualizing data-driven business insights to improve customer experiences

- Building cloud-native hyperscale applications and (API) platforms

Hence, it is quite evident as to why API-led architectures are the way forward for building enterprise applications.

The emergence of API-led architectures

The term **Application Programming Interfaces**, or **APIs**, was coined way back in the 1940s to establish some standardization in data formats, communication protocols, conventions to follow, and so on when different computing systems interacted with each other. Over time, API-based integration has become the *de facto* standard for interactions between applications, be it client-server or process-to-process communications.

In the new normal, enterprises rely heavily on APIs and microservices to build and connect applications. There has been a paradigm shift on the basic premise while building applications. Modern era experiences must aid in the following:

Simplifying the business processes: For example, in a retail kind of scenario, the tracking of inventoried items can be simplified by creating an API-based system over your inventory management system. These APIs can be consumed by different applications targeted at the store manager, point of sale, or back-office clerk to view and update the same.

- Improving the productivity of the workforce: For example, employees can make use of a variety of devices with apps that integrate with the backend APIs to get their work done. This will render them mobile while publishing real-time updates.

- Providing omnichannel access to customers: For example, customers today prefer to make use of both mobile and web apps to access any service or solutions.

- Achieving seamless data integration with channel partners and vendors: API-based integration platforms in the cloud allow easy integration and access to enterprise workflows.

- Ensuring data privacy and compliance: The standardization of IT policies, coupled with stricter governance over API platforms, plays a big role in preventing any security risks.

The core objective has always been to reduce complexities when dealing with people, processes, and tools within an enterprise.

The complexity problem

Large enterprises typically have multiple IT systems to cater to the need of various departments so as to support the different business processes. This typically leads to the creation of silos, requiring the duplication of data across different systems.

The focus of discussion of most enterprise architects is the integration between these systems and how to constantly evolve them to support the demands of the business. Considering that more than 80% of IT budgets are spent on maintaining and managing these large business systems, the **return on investment** (**ROI**) is highly dependent on the ease with which additional capabilities can be rolled out without impacting the existing rhythm of business.

APIs, being the basic building blocks of any digital footprint, act as a catalyst to reduce the complexity problem. APIs are relatively easy to develop and deploy. A good ecosystem of APIs within an enterprise can expedite the revenue generation process through the direct or indirect utilization of the underlying exposed data. Insights derived from data can serve as essential feedback to optimize both the business processes and associated IT systems.

The importance of API-led architecture

With data being the new currency for digital transformations, API-led architectures come to the rescue here. Almost all enterprises can be modeled as islands of discrete business capability, with some overlap for a cohesive operating model. This approach helps in defining the boundaries for the various systems and sub-systems that must be provisioned, and what interfaces must be developed to allow for data collection and exchange in a secured manner.

As the technology trends suggest, enterprises are increasingly adopting an API-led architecture strategy as it enables them to open their IT systems to external clients, business partners, and even third-party developers. The APIs serve as a black box, encapsulating all the business validations and rules that may apply to any process flow. In today's application development ecosystem, we find APIs everywhere, be it cloud computing services, productivity tools, or even on-premises integrations.

Consumers of the APIs simply reference the documented interfaces to develop their applications and services to transact with the respective systems, using the exposed APIs. For business owners, this simplifies the life cycle management of the solution, as the underlying logic for an API can be upgraded independently without breaking any upstream or downstream systems so long as the documented contract and data definitions do not change.

Hence, the key benefits of API-led architectures can be summarized as follows:

- Act as accelerators of cloud adoption within an enterprise.

- Provide the foundations for establishing an omnichannel strategy.

- Advance the decentralization of IT and business workflows.

- The generation of revenue through API economy.

The focus of the various chapters in this book is to show you how to get the benefits stated here and see how the adoption of various tactical strategies by your software development team may have a huge bearing on the success of your initiatives.

Case study

We will make use of the following case study to correlate and contextualize the concepts presented in subsequent chapters.

> **Note**
>
> This case study has been designed to simulate a real-world scenario. However, it is not meant to be comprehensive and exhaustive, catering to all business requirements or scenarios. The solutions and approach presented in the later stages are based on my point of view and should not be misconstrued as prescriptive guidance. Architecture and design is an evolving process and, hence, the reader is expected to build upon their existing understanding by working through this case study.

About Packt Insurance Inc.

Packt Insurance Inc, a company with a presence in over 10 countries (across America and Europe), offers a wide range of insurance products and services to its customers.

Over the last few years, the year-on-year growth of Packt Insurance has not been on a par with market opportunities. It is gradually receding to its competition due to a lack of market adaptability, high cycle time on innovation, and poor workforce productivity and collaboration owing to the use of legacy LOB applications for running the business. Its cloud presence is limited, and most of its applications are deployed as on-premises solutions.

In a recently concluded board meeting, a decision was taken to accelerate the company's digital transformation journey through its cloud adoption program. Packt Insurance wants to modernize even its LOB applications with a core priority of cloud-first and mobile-first approaches.

A summary of the key business drivers and stakeholder viewpoints is mentioned in the following section. For this case study, it is meant to demonstrate how each stakeholder perceives the business problem and their requirements for the target solution.

Key business drivers

- Become a cloud-based digital business within the next 2-3 years.
- Improve the speed to market, launching new services on a par with market trends.
- Expand operations in newer locations and geographies.

Stakeholder priorities

CEO:

- Achieve > 10-15% growth by expanding on product offerings, broadening distribution channels, and enhancing integration with channel partners.

CTO:

- I don't want to invest in IT infrastructure upfront, but rather spend incrementally as we expand the business.
- I want to know the profitability of our business units. I would appreciate some insights into our business that will enable me to make decisions.
- It would be great to know customer sentiments in terms of what they like about us and what they don't like.
- I would like to be known as a technology innovator/pioneer in the domain and attract the new tech-savvy generation.

IT operations:

- The adoption of modern practices for cloud-based solution development and deployment across the enterprise.
- Ensure compliance with security and data privacy standards.
- The onboarding of new branch offices should be quick and seamless.

Product manager:

- Reduce the cycle time of new insurance products from the current 6-8 months to a maximum of 2-3 months.

- It would be preferable if actuarial rules can be updated without any IT intervention.

Modernization roadmap

The executives at Packt Insurance have prioritized the roadmap for the different IT initiatives to modernize their core LOB application in three phases:

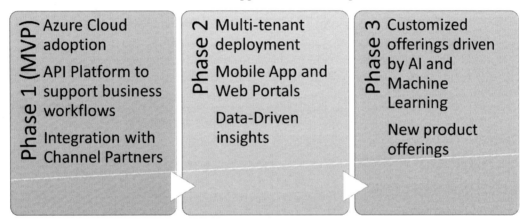

Figure 1.3 – A phased approach for digital transformation milestones

In the preceding diagram, the following applies:

- **Phase 1**: In this phase, the prioritized list of capabilities targeted for a **Minimum Viable Product** (**MVP**) will be developed. The objective of this phase is to quickly operationalize the first version of the platform.

- **Phase 2**: This is a continuation of *Phase 1*, and the next set of prioritized capabilities can be taken up. Typically in this phase, the first release of mobile apps and web portals will be targeted.

- **Phase 3**: This is the continuous innovation phase wherein AI and machine learning capabilities will be utilized to drive newer product offerings and improve the overall digital services deployed.

A simplistic business workflow

A very high-level flow diagram of business processes from an end-user perspective is provided here:

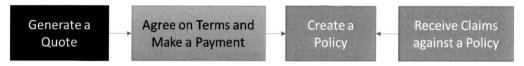

Figure 1.4 – A very high-level end-user flow

Packt Insurance Inc. is interested in the following business objectives:

- Maximize the conversion rate of quotes to users purchasing a policy. This is how the main revenue is generated. Hence, the premium amount quoted to customers should be comparable with other market players. Customers can evaluate the pros and cons, comparing the risk factors to decide whether to purchase a policy.

- Optimize the claim amount to improve the margin on policies. This is to ensure that the benefits extended are appropriate, but still come at a low cost to the company.

Summary

In this chapter, we have reviewed the importance of API-led architectures and how they are critical to the success of the digital vision of an enterprise. Every enterprise is different, having varying degrees of maturity in terms of their usage of IT for the running of the business. Hence, the focus of this chapter has been to establish some common principles that must be on the radar of the IT leaders of the organization. Digital transformations cannot be achieved through makeshift arrangements. It requires careful planning and ruthless prioritization to reap greater benefits fromthe investments made.

As revenue generation is the most important priority for any organization, this chapter highlighted the impact APIs can have within an enterprise, and what role they play in enabling transformation and agility vis-à-vis achieving business outcomes.

In the next chapter, we will understand how APIs act as digital connectors and their impact on the digital economy.

Further reading

- Eight reasons why architects love API-driven architectures: `https://hub.packtpub.com/architects-love-api-driven-architecture/`

- Microservices: An application revolution powered by the cloud: `https://azure.microsoft.com/en-us/blog/microservices-an-application-revolution-powered-by-the-cloud/`

- Microservices by Martin Fowler: `https://www.martinfowler.com/articles/microservices.html`

- What is API-Led – An Architectural Approach: `https://dzone.com/articles/what-is-api-led-an-architectural-approach-by-luis`

- Enterprise Architecture – Building a Robust Business IT Landscape: `https://medium.com/quick-code/enterprise-architecture-building-a-robust-business-it-landscape-e966edda102a`

- Build cloud-native applications in Azure: `https://azure.microsoft.com/en-in/overview/cloudnative/`

- Software as a Service (SaaS) concepts: `https://www.w3schools.in/cloud-services/software-as-a-service/`

2
APIs as Digital Connectors

APIs offer the ability to access information exposed by any system directly using a simple request-response mechanism without the need for a **user interface (UI)**. As they allow you to connect to a system, in a way similar to the plug and play model, they can be seen as **digital connectors**.

The **Connector** pattern is used in software engineering to enable network connectivity between communication endpoints, such as the client and the server. It is used in conjunction with the **Acceptor** pattern to enable network devices to evolve independently of the mechanisms that passively establish connections used by the services:

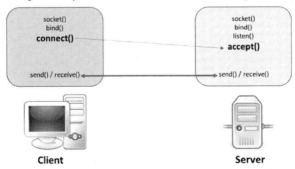

Figure 2.1 – A simplistic view of communication between machines using the Connector-Acceptor pattern

APIs are the modern world manifestation of the foundational blocks for these frontline connectivity touchpoints. Hence, it is important to treat APIs as digital assets of enterprise innovation, to reap the benefits of the transformation through a carefully designed API ecosystem.

The purpose of this chapter is to establish APIs as transformational digital channels for a modern enterprise. It also covers how **API-led connectivity** is reshaping the industry boundaries, and how newer methods of integration and distribution channels are broadening the IT landscape for enterprises.

This chapter also reflects upon the benefits of a well-connected enterprise and why traditional **service-oriented** approaches must be re-imagined to meet the connectivity needs of the present world as well as to prepare for the future through API-led architectures.

In this chapter, we are going to cover the following main topics:

- The connected enterprise
- The role of APIs in digital experiences
- An API is a digital service
- Packt Insurance Inc. – an API-led architecture strategy

By the end of this chapter, you will have a big picture view of the interactions and integrations that typically happen within an enterprise context, and how APIs can be viewed as the building blocks of your digital transformation strategy.

> **Did you know?**
>
> Gartner predicts that by 2025, 95% of the software application providers that consume cloud services as part of their product offerings will also market, sell, and provision their offerings through cloud platform marketplaces.

The connected enterprise

A **connected enterprise** is one where the business can truly connect with its customers, partners, and employees in a coherent manner to deliver business value at every step with greater productivity. A connected enterprise is always best suited to adapt quickly to industry changes. It applies market insights to pursue opportunities that drive innovation and growth. This, however, requires scrutiny of the existing systems and processes in place and then reimagining the business workflows to aim toward more sustainable growth.

The following diagram depicts how customer outcomes are tightly coupled with the efficiency and effectiveness with which other gears such as employees and partners are operating within an enterprise:

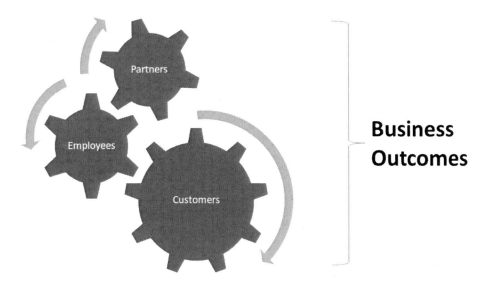

Figure 2.2 – The connected enterprise – synchronicity across customers, partners, and employees

In the next sections, we will look into the various ways in which API-led architectures drive the business outcomes of an enterprise.

The role of APIs in digital experiences

APIs have been around for a while, but their importance and compelling potential as crucial instruments of business execution were never understood before. They facilitate the seamless exchange of information across various systems. APIs also enable developers to build newer applications and digital experiences.

APIs are crucial to building digital experiences due to the following:

- They can be accessed from anywhere.
- They can be easily found in a central repository.
- They can comply with the latest security rules, such as GDPR.
- They can abstract backend data services from their consumers.
- They can be developed in any preferred programming language.
- They can control the throughput to protected backend services against DoS attacks.

Thus, it is a well-established fact that the **return on investment (ROI)** on API-led strategies is just phenomenal. Almost all organizations have started prioritizing their cloud initiatives toward accomplishing this goal.

Now you may wonder: "How do you calculate ROI?" In simple terms, the ROI for any IT strategy can be calculated as revenue generated minus the investment required. Let's look at the various cost and revenue buckets:

- **Investment**: Development costs, infrastructure costs, maintenance costs, revision/upgrade costs, and release costs

- **Revenue**: Income through customers and new opportunities (upselling/cross-selling)

API-led strategies that leverage the modern microservices architecture style aid in the following:

- A significant reduction in the revision and release costs

- Adapting to market demands and user voice, leading to greater loyalty and sustained growth of the customer base

- Having an edge over the competition by allowing new business opportunities, thereby boosting revenue growth

Considering these, it is only fair to state that the ROI for API-led strategies will be high (profitable) compared to any other approach.

Organizations that plan to adopt a robust API-led connectivity strategy will reap the benefits in the long term. These API platforms will add up to the **unique selling point (USP)** of enterprises when they transact with their partners and customers.

Major benefits of API-led connectivity

Organizations want to deliver the maximum experience to their customers and partners at a minimum investment. Hence, they want to be both flexible and adaptive in their solutions. This is where API-led connectivity plays a crucial part. Let's understand the major benefits of API-led connectivity.

An enriched customer experience

The bargaining power of customers drives enterprises toward building experiences that offer value for money. Simply put, customers prefer to buy from companies that offer an experience of their choice. Every customer is unique and has their own way of engaging with the businesses. By exposing business data as APIs, enterprises can exploit the opportunity of allowing developers, channel partners, and even customers to build engaging experiences having a personalized touch. Insights derived through the usage of **Artificial Intelligence (AI)** and **Machine Learning (ML)** can also be leveraged to further enrich the capabilities of these digital experiences.

Fostering connectivity and collaboration

Given any large enterprise, there could be easily 100+ apps for various purposes, some of which might even be legacy. APIs offer a way to integrate these siloed applications, thereby allowing cross-functional data exchange. This enhances the overall productivity and eventually improves the profitability of the enterprise along with the flexibility for changes and upgrades as and when required.

API-led connectivity strategies have led to the tremendous growth of **Business to Business (B2B)** collaboration scenarios. For example, in a supply chain kind of a scenario, the producer of finished goods can source the inventory of raw materials at the right time by opening their **Enterprise Resource Planning (ERP)** systems for API-based integrations with the corresponding partner or vendor. Automated and transparent tracking of orders and payments will eliminate any delays in the release of the inventory that may occur due to disconnected manual reconciliation between separate systems.

Further, it is only prudent to state that API-led connectivity offers the best seamless integration across enterprises that may have their own tools and technologies to run the business at their end. B2B **enterprise application integration (EAI)** workflows can be easily developed using the industry-standard data exchange formats, using supported protocols.

> **Note**
> EAI and B2B scenarios will be covered in more detail in *Chapter 8, API-Centric Enterprise Integrations*.

Fueling growth through innovation

Decoupling user experiences from the backend business logic and data opens a wide range of possibilities for an enterprise. Platform developers can focus on building APIs that serve as layers of abstraction over the business data, whereas frontend or client application developers can innovate on the end user experiences, thereby allowing them to meet the dynamics of the market, customer, and technology trends.

With APIs, companies can expedite their innovation journeys to improve the speed to market and strengthen their competitive advantage in the industry.

APIs serve as digital enablers for an enterprise

Considering the benefits of API-led connectivity as described in the previous section, APIs can be considered as digital enablers for an enterprise.

They allow an enterprise to do the following:

- Focus on the overall strategy and business goals
- Increase the digital reach of the services offered
- Achieve the business results
- Offer data-driven insights for effective decision making

An API is a digital service

Businesses are finding different ways to use data and services for competitive leverage. The most important interaction touchpoint for customers and consumers alike is the **published API layer**. From plain vanilla API platforms to **Integration Platform as a Service (iPaaS)**, organizations are expanding their digital footprint of these API-led architectures.

Most enterprises have already embarked on a journey to design and adopt an API-led architecture strategy to survive against the competition. Start-ups are already leveraging technology to its fullest potential to attract and wow their customer base. Hence, traditional businesses cannot afford to stay far behind in their journeys to avoid losing out on their market share.

API architecture within an enterprise

While the actual implementation of an API architecture may vary between organizations, the segregation and grouping of APIs through a logical architecture can be broadly depicted as mentioned here:

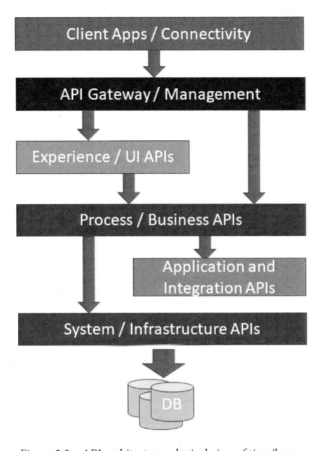

Figure 2.3 – API architecture – logical view of tiers/layers

Client apps/connectivity

This tier comprises all the applications (internal and external) that integrate with the various APIs for the delivery of end user experiences and associated business functionality. Typically, these would be *mobile/web/desktop apps* and even backend services of other external applications that are hosted elsewhere. These clients connect and exchange data as per the published data and service contracts using the protocol and connectivity options supported by the API platform.

API gateway or management

The **API gateway** serves as the single entry point and offers a standardized process for all interactions between the clients and the API. It also serves as a management layer for discovery, usage, and other important functions such as authentication, authorization, throttling, message translation, and transformation and monitoring.

Experience APIs

These are the set of APIs that are required to propel the **user interface (UI)** of **client apps**. These APIs are designed to provide a layer of abstraction to decouple presentation data models from the underlying storage data model. These APIs are generally lightweight and should not contain any major business logic apart from schema validations to ensure that proper data is received from the clients for the execution of the underlying business workflows through the process APIs.

These APIs are primarily used for multi-channel delivery.

Business or process APIs

These APIs contain the business logic and rules that may apply to the processing of a request. These are separated out to ensure that the rules are consistently followed irrespective of the entry point, and the data remains in a consistent state after being processed.

These APIs are typically heavyweight, and highly dependent on the nature and criticality of the business workflow. Hence, these APIs must be carefully designed to ensure maintainability and extensibility. It is also advisable to keep the rules flexible so that they can be changed easily without incurring high maintenance costs.

Application and integration APIs

These APIs are usually invoked during **Enterprise Application Integration (EAI)** scenarios. They contain logic to transform the data model consumed from the source into a canonical model that will be supported by the systems under integration. Thus, integration APIs can act as a mediator on behalf of other applications or systems in the enterprise.

System or infrastructure APIs

These APIs serve as the connectivity blocks for the underlying data store. These are also known as **data services**. These APIs ensure that direct access to a data store is not possible from the systems, and only standard access patterns that are permitted can be used. These APIs also serve as a repository layer, to encapsulate the underlying storage implementation from the higher tiers so that it is easier to change or upgrade the storage tier without impacting any already working applications. Generally, this layer requires the most careful consideration as it works with the store directly, and proper security controls must be in place to avoid any data breach or even malicious access.

Database, the persistent store

This serves as the persistence tier of the solution. These are typically various storage solutions (blobs, RDMS, NoSQL, or even SaaS products). You can find a large footprint of various storage technologies within an enterprise.

API classification by management and access pattern

APIs within an enterprise can be broadly classified as follows:

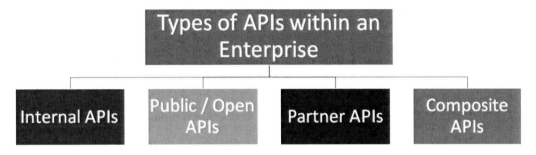

Figure 2.4 – Types of APIs within an enterprise

Let's take a detailed look at each type of API to understand its intended purpose and use.

Internal APIs

This is the most common use case within an enterprise. Internal or private APIs are used for information exchange within the various silos within an enterprise, or even to power client-side mobile or web apps. The decoupling of the business layer (APIs) from the presentation logic (*UI apps*) provides the ability to build great end user experiences. These APIs must be highly secure, follow an authorization framework, and must adhere to the corporate security policies to prevent any data breaches.

Typical examples of internal APIs are the following:

- APIs for ERP systems such as SAP and TIBCO that will be consumed by other business applications, such as point-of-sale and the online store
- APIs for shared services such as email or SMS so that all applications can make use of a common gateway for the delivery of messages
- Exposing on-premises hosted backend HTTP services to be consumed by line-of-business cloud applications

Public APIs

Public APIs support consumer access for business purposes. Typically, they are available for use by authorized developers or enterprises for integration in their custom application scenarios. Public APIs may require an active subscription (or keys) for access as they might be chargeable on a *pay-per-use model*. Some public APIs might also be free and open to use by anyone.

Public APIs may be secured and require authentication and authorization as well. Hence, security threats (if any) apply equally to these types of APIs as well.

Public APIs can be free or charged. A few practical examples are as follows:

- Exposing datasets that can be consumed by the general public, for example, COVID-related data by various government agencies
- API services that are offered to consumers, for example, geo-location or mapping services from Microsoft or Google, or email or SMS sending services by Twilio

(External) partner APIs

Partner APIs are used to support integration with authorized external channel partners only. The most common requirement is the integration with any backend ERP system of an enterprise that is not exposed to the outside world. Additionally, the nature of line-of-business applications may vary across various enterprises, and hence a common and standardized data exchange mechanism must be developed for the seamless integration of the data islands that may exist.

The partner APIs are designed for specific purposes only and may support a variety of protocols and data formats that are required for the bi-directional integrations to work.

Partner APIs are primarily developed to support Enterprise Application Integration scenarios. Hence, typical examples include APIs that can support various integration flows. This is covered in more detail in *Chapter 8, API-Centric Enterprise Integrations*.

Composite APIs

These APIs serve as aggregators by combining the output from multiple internal APIs into a single response. They are mostly used in a **Façade** layer kind of a pattern or even **backend for frontend (BFF) patterns**.

Composite APIs are beneficial in scenarios wherein the performance of the user interaction for client-side apps must be improved by avoiding a chatty interface. Each network call will incur some latency, thereby impacting the overall performance of the user scenario and steps required to accomplish a task.

Composite APIs are used when building frontend applications that have a different view model for the UI depending on the type of client.

For example, for a business entity that has 10 fields in the backend, a mobile app may show only 4 fields, whereas a web app can show all 10 fields due to the available screen size and form factor. Hence, a facade or wrapper API will be developed that controls the amount of data sent to the client based on its type.

Packt Insurance Inc. – an API-led architecture strategy

The development team at Packt Insurance already knew the fact that building a robust Azure cloud-based API platform would make them future-ready. They can drive future innovation and customer engagement by building best-in-class experience apps. They can apply AI and ML to improve their product offerings. They can leverage the scale of the cloud to expand their business.

The approach and the concepts presented in the following sections will help you understand how to identify the boundaries of a complex enterprise solution and how to model the high-level business workflows, keeping in context the touchpoints of the various persona types. This aids in visualizing a big picture view of the various API requirements and their respective categorization. Modern API-led architectures are primarily microservices-driven. Hence, this case study also suggests the approach to defining API blocks for the microservices. Structurally, a microservice can contain one or many discrete API blocks.

Domain decomposition

The development team decided to build a microservices-based architecture for their API platform strategy. The team applied **domain-driven design (DDD)** techniques to identify the high-level business subdomains of the insurance domain.

> **DDD**
>
> DDD is a concept introduced by a programmer named Eric Evans in 2004, in his book *Domain-Driven Design: Tackling Complexity in the Heart of Software*. It is an approach for architecting software design by looking at software in a top-down approach.
>
> You are advised to read about the concepts of DDD to improve your understanding of the subject and the terms that are used.

An insurance domain comprises various sub domains, such as insurance products, rates and rules, quotes, policies, claims, customers, business application users (identity), invoices and payments, and marketing promotions.

The following diagram depicts the boundaries of the various sub-domains and their relationship using the dotted lines:

> **Note**
>
> This is just an initial list for illustration purposes only. However, the actual list of subdomains could be longer and will vary based on the nature of the company.

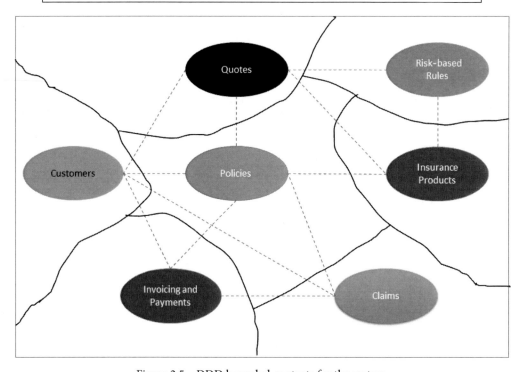

Figure 2.5 – DDD bounded contexts for the system

Service and persona map

A high-level view of the **service** and **persona** map is depicted here:

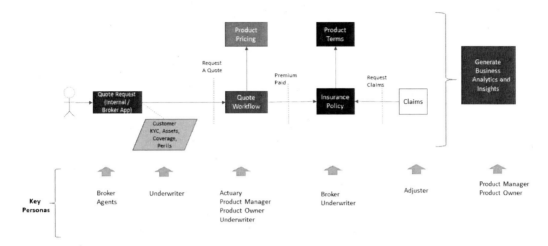

Figure 2.6 – Service and persona map

The preceding diagram depicts the high-level boundaries of the various services (or sub-systems) that have to be developed, and how the data and interactions will happen as part of the business workflow.

> **Note**
>
> In the preceding depiction, only the key persona types have been considered that will have a bearing on the design of the API platform. End users/customers have not been considered as they will make use of the mobile/web apps to interact with the system.

Persona descriptions are provided here:

Persona	Description
Brokers/Agents	They act as intermediaries between prospective customers and insurance companies and typically assist in explaining the various insurance product offerings, their benefits, and also support in filling out the necessary paperwork (online/offline).
	This is purely for the purpose of requesting a quote and then subsequently pursuing the customer to purchase a policy.
Underwriters	Insurance underwriters perform two functions.
	One, they evaluate the risk implied by an applicant to determine whether to accept or reject an application. If assuming the chance favors such an insurer, they accept it. Subsequently, they set a premium reflecting such a perceived risk and outline the guidelines for an applicant.
	Second, they review claims submitted by policyholders. Based on their evaluation, underwriters decide whether a claim is legitimate or not. If consistent, they determine the appropriate coverage amount.
Adjusters	The job of an insurance adjuster is to assess the claim made by the customer against the risks and coverage as part of the terms of the policy. They compute the eligible loss incurred by the policyholder and adjust the claim amount before the actual payout happens. They ensure that claims are legitimate and do not result in a substantial loss for the insurance company.
Actuary	An actuary is a professional who specializes in the field of analyzing financial risks by implementing statistical, financial, and mathematical theories.
	The job of an actuary is critical. On the one hand, they need to ensure that the policy amount quoted to a customer is optimal as per the risk factors involved with the policy, while on the other, they need to ensure that proper analysis is done on the coverage aspects to derive the right price to ensure good profitability for the insurance company.
Product Manager	Product managers typically have a thorough understanding of the organization's overall vision and priorities. They typically work with the key internal stakeholders (primarily the leadership team) to define the roadmaps and strategies to introduce a portfolio of insurance products to improve the profitability of the company.
Product Owner	The role of the product owner is to balance out the priorities and define the tactical release plans involving product backlog prioritization based on feedback and inputs received.
	They also make use of analytics derived from the data to prioritize the initiatives/projects and expedite the development of IT solutions for them. The product owner also serves the dual purpose of a program manager for the IT team of the organization.

Why is this important?

The study of the various persona types is extremely important to research their existing pain points purely from an enterprise context. Any systems designed must address these pain points for eventual adoption and usage. As we learned in the *The connected enterprise* section, employees and partners are important stakeholders to achieve business outcomes.

So, you must capture the comprehensive list of users who may have a direct impact on the requirements of the solution being envisaged.

API composability using microservices

As you start detailing out the sub-systems for the various bounded contexts, along with identification of the various business operations, the list of microservices starts emerging along with identification of the APIs that must be created. Some of these APIs will be public or external, while others will be internal or composite in nature.

The composition of the various microservice boundaries using API blocks is depicted here:

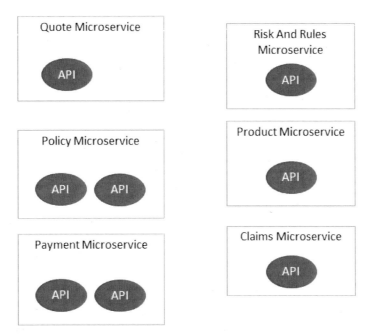

Figure 2.7 – API composability using microservices for the insurance domain

As a follow-up exercise, you may want to try listing out the various APIs and their corresponding operations. Apply the principles of domain-driven design to find business entities, relations, state transitions, and events.

Event storming is a useful technique to identify the domain boundaries and create a high-level context map for the various microservices.

> **Note**
>
> The DDD-based approach was selected due to its wide usage in the industry as a popular standard. Every business system can be easily expressed using a domain model and the business functions can be interpreted as behaviors of the domain model. This simplifies the design of the code-level components by providing an object-oriented way of defining the interfaces, classes, and data objects. Additionally, developers can follow the principles of **Behavior-Driven Design (BDD)** during the implementation phases to ensure the overall correctness of the functionality.
>
> However, it does require a good understanding of the concepts before teams are ready to apply the DDD pattern. Hence, development teams can also take a look at other industry practices to expedite the API design work.

Summary

In this chapter, we have reviewed how APIs are increasingly being used as a valuable and powerful asset to offer versatile connectivity experiences for digital enterprises. The adoption of open specification standards has reduced the complexities of building integrations.

Developers can build APIs in the language of their choice but still achieve seamless connectivity and usage by the API consumers. Cloud-based providers are investing heavily to support EAI integrations, which comprise more than 80% of all enterprise integration scenarios. As legacy platforms are fading out, enterprises are investing heavily in building next-generation highly secure integration platforms on the cloud.

You can make use of the concepts presented in this chapter and analyze your organization context to identify the different APIs that may exist. Also, check whether you are able to identify the opportunities for your business to build additional API platforms for greater engagement.

Great API design is an architectural concern as it combines the business drivers with product capabilities and a software solution approach. Hence, it is critical that you plan to implement a robust API-led architecture for the success of the digital platform.

In the next chapter, we will look at some of the important architecture principles and styles that must be adopted while building highly scalable and reliable API-centric solutions.

Further reading

- Top Priorities for Tech & Service Providers: Leadership Vision for 2021 (gartner.com): `https://www.gartner.com/en/publications/top-priorities-for-tech-service-providers-leadership-vision-2021`

- Guide to building an enterprise API strategy (techtarget.com): `https://searchapparchitecture.techtarget.com/Guide-to-building-an-enterprise-API-strategy`

- Designing a "DDD-Oriented" Microservice: `https://docs.microsoft.com/en-us/dotnet/architecture/microservices/microservice-ddd-cqrs-patterns/ddd-oriented-microservice`

- What is Behavior-Driven Design?: `https://www.agilealliance.org/glossary/bdd`

Section 2:
Build Reliable
API-Centric Solutions

The second part of this book covers the design considerations that are important for building robust and scalable API-centric solutions for the cloud, with a focus on the important tactical practices that are required to meet the expected business outcomes, as measured through tracked metrics.

This section includes the following chapters:

- *Chapter 3, Architecture Principles and API Styles*
- *Chapter 4, Assuring the Quality of the API Service (or Product)*
- *Chapter 5, RESTFul API – the New Web Standard*
- *Chapter 6, API Design Practices*
- *Chapter 7, Accelerating through DevOps Essentials*

3
Architecture Principles and API Styles

Architecture principles are a set of general rules and guidelines that are meant to serve as the core tenets for the design, development, and maintenance of IT solutions within an enterprise. These principles are meant to govern the decision-making process throughout the life cycle stages of an application to accomplish the goals outlined by the organization.

The purpose of this chapter is to review the key architecture principles that will apply to API-centric solutions, and how they translate into the product backlog.

The chapter also presents some of the industry-standard API architecture styles along with references to Azure cloud-based implementation techniques.

In this chapter, we are going to cover the following main topics:

- Architecture principles
- Evolve architecture blueprints iteratively
- Constructs of an API
- Popular API architecture styles

- Finding the right style for your API use cases

- Serverless APIs – accelerators for innovation

- Implementing API-led architectures in Azure

- Case study elaboration – Packt Insurance Inc.

By the end of this chapter, you will be familiar with the intricacies of the various architectural styles and decide on what best suits your API platform needs. You will also be adept in making fit-for-purpose decisions by choosing the right Azure services to build highly scalable and resilient APIs on Azure.

> **Tip**
> Architecture backlog must be prioritized alongside functional backlog to deliver a highly reliable and scalable API service.

Architecture principles

The foundation to building a highly reliable API-centric architecture is to focus on the core objectives and goals that must be addressed by the solution for the given context. This is typically outlined using a list of *architecture principles* that serve as the guiding principle for solution architects and engineers while they analyze the requirements of the business and prepare the implementation roadmap for the solution.

Some of the standard software architecture principles are must-have for API architectures as well. . A few others are based on modern practices that are more relevant for cloud-based solutions.

The most important architecture principles that commonly apply to API platforms are categorized as follows:

- **Keep it simple**: Minimize moving parts to reduce complexity and accelerate the time to market. In the world of Agile and iterative development, changes are expected as a natural process. Trying to get the architecture right and comprehensive from the very outset is sometimes almost impossible. Hence, allow the API platform architecture to just evolve organically as and when clarity is received through backlog elaboration.

- **Fit for purpose**: Adequately address key requirements (must-haves) of various stakeholders so that it can be implemented within a reasonable time frame. Leverage the **Architecture Trade-off Analysis Method** (**ATAM**) to derive the right balance among the competing priorities. For more details on ATAM, refer to the following link: `https://www.geeksforgeeks.org/architecture-tradeoff-analysis-method-atam/`.

- **Right tool/solution for the task**: Architecture should, as per the problem statement, infer best practices and reference architectures. A fit-gap study must be conducted to understand the benefits of one approach over the other, and the results captured as the basis of your architecture decision. In a rapidly evolving technology landscape, newer technologies/products may reduce your customization needs.

- **Divide and conquer (separating responsibilities)**: These are loosely coupled, independently deployable components that are highly maintainable and testable. This is key while building microservices. Each API must serve a specific purpose and their life cycles can be managed independently of other APIs in the platform.

- **Prepare for failure**: Systems should be fault-tolerant and recover from failures quickly. Transient faults are expected from any cloud-based solution. Hence, the system must plan for it and offer greater reliability.

- **Secure by design**: Security is the most important aspect of any architecture. Implement the principles of defense in depth to ensure that the solution is protected at all layers.

- **Cost optimal but delivers business value**: Business outcomes must be realized with reasonable investments. Businesses operate on profit, and so even if they like it, they won't have the budget to procure expensive resources. The solution envisaged must be financially viable for the business.

- **Measure what's important**: Derive actionable insights from the logs/metrics captured. Feedback loops are important for continuous improvement. There must be adequate instrumentation and logging strategies in a plan so that administrators/business owners can receive tangible insights to take decisions.

- **Design for high availability/design for self-healing**: Anticipate, plan, and gracefully recover from failures without significantly impacting user experiences. Solutions must bake in automation to detect failures and prefer automated failover over healthy instances to minimize downtime.

- **Think serverless, PaaS over IaaS**: Focus on the solution, and let the cloud manage your infrastructure required to run it. Wherever possible, plan to build lightweight and flexible, yet highly scalable, services that can be deployed or upgraded easily. Later in this chapter, you will get an expanded view of the concept of using serverless technologies for building APIs.

> **Note**
> The list of architecture principles captured earlier in this chapter is typically the most important focus area for the majority of cloud-based solutions. However, it is not meant to be an exhaustive list, and additional principles may apply to your context.

Evolve architecture blueprints iteratively

Architecture blueprints are typically a set of diagrams and supporting documentation that provides a high-level view of the solution being envisaged from a conceptual, logical, and physical or deployment point of view. It captures the relationship between the various components along with the interaction and integration patterns, bearing in mind the various functional and architecture requirements of the solution.

Traditionally, IT architects have followed a *big bang* kind of approach, attempting to finalize most parts of the architecture before starting any development work. The primary goal was to identify most of the risks upfront, and then mitigate them before any significant investment of time was done. However, in recent times, the approach for the architecture definition process has shifted from this conventional big bang style to a more *experiment, learn, and improve model*:

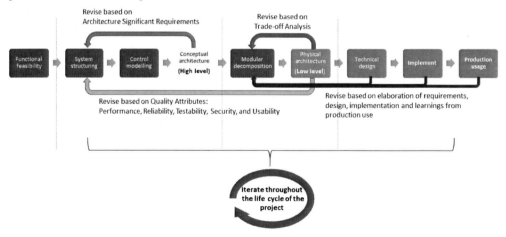

Figure 3.1 – Agile Architecture evolution process

The steps depicted in the preceding diagram are briefly described here:

Step	Description/Activities
Functional Feasibility	Identify key business drivers, goals, and scenarios.
	Assess the technical feasibility of the solution.
System Structuring	Systems structuring refers to how the system is decomposed into several principal subsystems (or building blocks) and communications between those subsystems are then identified.
Control Modeling	Model the business processes and workflows using the building blocks of the solution.
Conceptual Architecture (High-Level)	Prepare the high-level solution architecture.
	This should cater to both the functional and non-functional requirements of the system.
Modular Decomposition	Modular decomposition is how we break down a system into smaller subsystems and identify their respective boundaries.
	During this step, we also make technology choices for implementing each subsystem, including identification of the dependencies between the various subsystems.
Physical Architecture (Low-Level)	Prepare the physical architecture, including the wiring diagram, of the respective physical resources.
Technical Design	Identify any constraints during design and use that as feedback to revise the architecture.
Implement	Improve the architecture based on discovery during the implementation of business scenarios.
Production Usage	Incorporate learnings from production use as backlog to revise the architecture.

Table 3.1 – Steps involved in the Agile Architecture evolution process

As is evident from the preceding section, solution architects and developers must adopt a more *continuous architecture mindset* where change is the only constant. While building API-first architectures, the same concepts apply. The team must focus on releasing a **Most Viable Product** (**MVP**) as soon as possible and then devise a prioritization strategy to release features and capabilities incrementally over time.

You can read more about Agile Architecture concepts here: `https://www. scaledagileframework.com/agile-architecture`.

Additionally, refer to this link for continuous architecture principles: `https://resources.sei.cmu.edu/asset_files/ Presentation/2016_017_001_454847.pdf`.

Constructs of an API

Before we start discussing the various architecture styles, let's get familiar with the different constructs that make up an API. Throughout this chapter, we will be using these terms and hence it is important to have a common understanding of them. The various parts that constitute an API are depicted here:

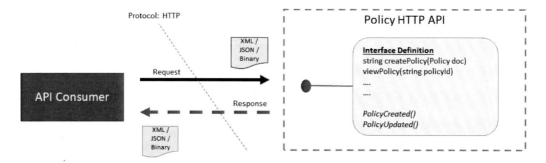

Figure 3.2 – Constructs of an API

The constructs of an API are explained in the following sections.

API operations or service contract

The **interface definition** of an API outlines the list of operations supported by the API. Each operation must be unique and should perform a single function or task; in other words, it follows the **single-responsibility principle**.

Data contract or entity schema

The data contract defines the schema of the entities that participate in the various operations supported by the API. The entities can be simple or complex data types depending on the type of operation being performed.

API endpoint

API endpoint refers to the published networking endpoint for the API. Depending on the hosting of the API service, the endpoint may be accessible over the internet, intranet, or even be private to a particular machine.

Communication protocol (application layer)

The communication protocol assists two software systems in conversing with one other. For this book, we will be focusing primarily on the communication protocols used in cloud computing, which are **Hypertext Transfer Protocol (HTTP)**, **Message Queuing Telemetry Transport (MQTT)**, and **Advanced Message Queuing Protocol (AMQP)**.

HTTP is very popular for web-based synchronous communication scenarios, whereas AMQP is used for message-oriented asynchronous interactions. MQTT is frequently used for machine-to-cloud communications.

Input and output – the request-response pair

While invoking an API, depending on the definition of the operation, the API consumers must send input data that will be processed at the server. Subsequently, a response as an output of the operation will be sent back to the caller.

For an HTTP-based interaction, the input can be specified using either HTTP headers, query string parameters, or even the request body. Here is an example of a simple HTTP GET request with a policy ID in the query string. The service will return the corresponding policy document in JSON format as a response to this request:

```
GET /policy/getPolicy?id=POLICY1122334455 HTTP/1.1
Host: api.contoso.inc
```

The resulting JSON response for this API may look something like this:

```
{
  "policyid": "POLICY1122334455",
   "startdate":"2020-03-03T00:00:00",
   "expirydate":" 2021-03-03T00:00:00",
   "customerid":"123456789",
   "details": {
      "product":"healthPlus",
       "term":"2",
```

```
        ...


        ...


    }
}
```

> **The HTTP standard**
>
> For a detailed understanding of the request-response pairs supported by
> the HTTP communication protocol, refer to the relevant W3C standards at
> `https://www.w3.org/Protocols/`.

Popular API architecture styles

API developers tend to use one or more API architecture styles based on the business
functionality and simplicity in implementation:

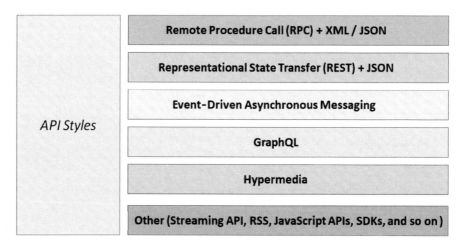

Figure 3.3 – Frequently used API styles

The commonly used styles are explained in the next sections.

The tunneling or RPC style

The tunneling, or **Remote Procedure Call** (**RPCs**), style is the oldest architecture style and
has been widely used for building API interfaces. The RPC style follows the client-server
model, wherein the server exposes a set of endpoints that serve as remote functions:

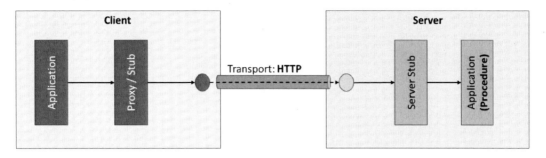

Figure 3.4 – RPC style

The clients interact with these endpoints using a well-defined message format organized using XML. Both the request body and response output of these APIs are in XML. This style is supported by a wide range of transport and communication standards, such as HTTP, TCP/IP, and JMS. The APIs may use encryption and decryption techniques to support message-level security as well. **JavaScript Object Notation (JSON)** data schemas can also be used for the request body and response output for RPC-style APIs.

The **Simple Object Access Protocol (SOAP)** API format is the most popular implementation of this style. The message format in SOAP adheres to the **Web Service Descriptive Language (WSDL)** standards, and so is slightly different from the generic RPC style. RPC-style APIs still prevail and are widely used in various business contexts.

A summary of the benefits and limitations is provided here:

Benefits	Limitations
• This style has been around for a while and the developer community is familiar with it. • Many legacy applications continue to use it. • This style is preferred for developing specialized operations for point-to-point performance.	• Was not originally designed for HTTP, and hence does not support all HTTP features, such as caching. • Not preferred for mobile or web applications requiring highly interactive applications. • Due to tight coupling between clients and servers, any changes incur high maintenance costs.

RI (or REST) style

The URI API style is also popularly known as the REST API style. It relies on the concept of invoking requests using HTTP operations to support different functions such as Create, Read, Update, and Delete on the business objects. It allows the requesting clients to invoke and manipulate web resources using standard HTTP protocol functions, thereby following a uniform convention that is easy to understand:

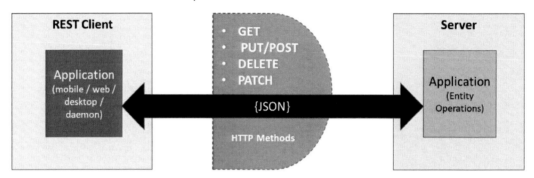

Figure 3.5 – REST API architecture

The APIs developed using this style are typically lightweight, easy to extend, and hence are mostly used for building public APIs, even backend APIs for mobile and web apps, to expose services and data over HTTP.

> **Tip**
> API applications that are protected by a web application firewall may require careful analysis of the API syntax for **Open Web Application Security Project (OWASP)** rules. Some of the query string parameters (especially for ODATA APIs) may be blocked as a result of suspecting SQL injection or scripting attacks. Hence, the RPC + JSON style might serve better for those scenarios.

A summary of the benefits and limitations is provided here:

Benefits	Limitations
• Uses the HTTP Verb, Path, and Query standards, allowing for ease of development. • Best suited for entity-based operations or data services. • Preferred API style for modern architectures and, hence a lot of guidance and tooling support is available for developers.	• Requires discipline while defining route paths for the CRUD operations. • The interface can be quite chatty depending on the user interactions on the data. • Must support backward compatibility as otherwise, API changes will break the clients.

Query or GraphQL style

The GraphQL API style is an extension of the REST API style and was developed as an alternative to improve the overall performance and efficiency of querying and retrieving results from a data source. The specification defines a format that is hierarchical and serves as documentation of your data needs.

This API style is used only for read purposes and is preferred when the queries on the data are a little complex and may require multiple calls using the standard REST operations. The two main building blocks for GraphQL are schema and query:

- **Schema**: A typed schema is used as API input. This schema captures the selection of fields of an object that you want to query.

- **Query**: This defines how to query the underlying data objects to fetch the right datasets with the highest accuracy for the information desired.

A summary of the benefits and limitations is provided here:

Benefits	Limitations
• This is the preferred style for data-centric apps. • The query style can be standardized using domain entities, and so is easier to implement using different technologies. • Client and server interactions are simple as they rely on query patterns to retrieve the data.	• A query schema is dependent on the underlying data model. Upgrades to a data model impact clients. • Use is limited to query-style APIs only. • Query performance must be modeled and planned to avoid slow queries at runtime.

Event-driven or asynchronous messaging style

Event-driven architectures have become quite popular in recent years as they can address classical concerns regarding reliability while building highly scalable APIs. This architecture style operates through the asynchronous messaging technique, whereby clients send messages to the server in a fire-and-forget pattern instead of request/reply. As the processing of the message happens outside of the main execution request flow, it is widely used for building responsive applications. There are multiple ways in which the final status of the message can be relayed to the client.

This is a powerful design style and supports a wide variety of transport and message-level protocols. Using this style, large data transfers are also possible. The messages posted to these APIs are first stored in intermediate messaging queues also known as **transient stores**. The subscribers to these queues typically contain the business logic that must be applied to process the received message and then transform and finally save it in the final target data repository (persistent store). Using the Publish-Subscribe pattern (for example, Message Broker), additional data processing pipelines can be implemented to operate on the received message simultaneously.

This style is commonly used in **Internet of Things** (**IoT**) scenarios, wherevic devices (de event producers) send a lot of telemetry messages to the cloud (event consumer).

However, one drawback of this style is that it adds some overall complexity while building highly intuitive interactions using mobile or web apps. Furthermore, it also requires additional hardware due to the additional layer of transient stores and message brokers. Hence, careful planning must be undertaken to remodel any legacy business flows before using this pattern.

A summary of the benefits and limitations is provided here:

Benefits	Limitations
• Loose coupling among applications. • High reliability due to asynchronous processing on the server. • User experience and navigation are improved significantly. • Integration interfaces can be simple and centralized.	• Suitable for building near-real-time applications only. • Increase in the complexity of the server solution architecture to ensure the guaranteed delivery of messages.

Hypermedia style

The hypermedia API architectural style is an extension to the REST architectural style, with the added capability of using hypermedia as its foundation of design. This style is largely used while building adaptive mobile or web apps.

Traditional RPC style, or even REST APIs, introduces a bit of tight coupling as the frontend apps must know which operations to invoke for the various screens. Hypermedia APIs, on the other hand, offer the benefit of producing their own URI paths for various operations supported on the data entity. Hence, developers building apps rely on the data to decide on the actions to be supported, thereby making the experience more adaptive. These dynamic URI linking concepts make these APIs interesting, as the consumer applications will not be impacted by any changes in the underlying workflow steps.

A summary of the benefits and limitations is provided here:

Benefits	Limitations
• Loosely coupled applications; changes are relatively easier to deploy. • HTTP only, and hence makes full use of the web-based APIs.	• Requires a lot of upfront planning to design the APIs properly. • The response messages can be verbose depending on the data. • Clients can be a little complex to design and develop.

Other API styles

There are a few other API styles that fit specific contexts. However, their usage is very limited and not very common in an enterprise context:

- **JavaScript APIs:** These are popular with browser web extensions and typically used for running background jobs or other intended actions.

- **Language Bindings or SDKs: Software Development Kits (SDKs)** are used for building applications targeted at a specific runtime or software package. The SDKs can contain APIs that serve as wrappers over any existing available services.

- **RSS and ATOM: Really Simple Syndication (RSS)** has been there for a while for the distribution of news feeds. **ATOM** is an enriched version of RSS feeds and is also used for the publishing of periodic information to its subscribers.

- **Streaming APIs:** These are used for sending information in chunks to the client instead of a single request-response pair. They are widely used for the live streaming of media files:

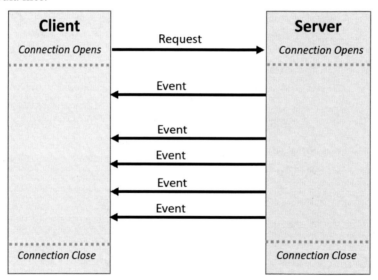

Figure 3.6 – Streaming API behavior

Finding the right style for your API use cases

When it comes to building API platforms, there is no one-size-fits-all. While certain styles are more modern and widely used, but each style has its limitations as well. Hence, the API development teams must evaluate the key scenarios carefully and apply some sort of weighted matrix to understand the pros and cons in order to determine the best style for the specific use case.

There is a usual tendency among developers to make use of experience and programming language familiarity while approaching API requirements for any newer projects. However, this approach is fraught with challenges when it comes to the extensibility of API platforms. So, you must always do a thorough analysis to select the right style for your needs.

You may want to consider the following guidance while selecting the API style for your use cases:

Use Case Scenario	Key Attributes	Preferred API Style
Management API	• Focus on data objects or resources • Different types of clients (web or mobile) • Should have discoverability and documentation	REST
Command API	• Action-oriented • Simple interactions, but data in the payload • Web service style of request-response pairs	RPC
Microservices	• High message rates • Both async and synchronous • Low overhead	RPC, REST, or Event Messaging
Read-only data query API	• Data is graph-like • Optimized for high latency	GraphQL
Media Streaming	• Streaming of multi-media content	Streaming API
Backend for Single-Page Applications	• Collections of entities with navigation to detailed views	Hypermedia
Enterprise Application Integrations (EAI)	• Loosely coupled interfaces • Integration by exchange of messages in supported formats	Event Messaging, RPC

The preceding list of use cases is not comprehensive and is provided as guidance only.

Serverless APIs – accelerators for innovation

Serverless computing is an execution model where the cloud provider (AWS, Azure, or Google Cloud) will dynamically allocate resources to run a block of deployed code. As the cloud provider manages the infrastructure, it will only charge for the resources utilized to run the code. Hence, customers will primarily be charged based on their usage.

You can read more about the Azure serverless offerings and their corresponding pricing models here: `https://azure.microsoft.com/en-us/solutions/serverless/`.

Serverless computing abstracts out the underlying infrastructure required to host and run any application. This enables developers to focus on building the applications without worrying about managing the server infrastructure. With serverless computing, the cloud service provider will manage the deployment and availability of the resources along with scaling based on demand.

Azure Functions, Logic App, Azure Kubernetes Services, and API Management are examples of serverless computing technologies of the Azure cloud that are covered in more detail in subsequent sections.

Benefits of using serverless computing for APIs

The prime benefits of using serverless computing are as follows:

- **Cloud-native and fully managed services**: With serverless computing, developers can shift their focus to building the business logic rather than spending cycles on managing the underlying infrastructure. Also, the deployment model is straightforward as you can easily deploy your code and run it.

- **Faster time to market**: Serverless computing reduces the operation's overhead and cycle time to deploy services in the cloud. Hence, the development teams can quickly build, deploy, and run the services. It also offers great agility to upgrade any existing solution.

- **On-demand scalability and high performance**: With serverless computing, the infrastructure can be scaled up or down based on demand. These automatic scaling capabilities also come with higher performance and availability of the platform. As the cloud provider manages resources, service scalability is managed automatically as per the configurations applied to it.

- **Cost optimization through the efficient use of resources**: This is perhaps the most important benefit of serverless computing. Organizations want to maximize the **total cost of ownership** (**TCO**) through the most optimal use of cloud resources. Serverless resources deployed with a consumption-based plan/tier are successful in ensuring the most efficient use of resources, thereby impacting the overall cost of running the solutions.

Hence, considering the key benefits, API developers can quickly create and deploy lightweight applications using serverless technologies to test out any new functionalities or experiment with features. The approach keeps costs minimal while circumventing the need for complex deployment procedures.

Serverless architecture use cases

Typical use cases of serverless architecture are as follows:

- Developers want to experiment with functionality and code without worrying about managing infrastructure to run them.

- Event/stream processing jobs, IoT data processing jobs, real-time processing jobs, and so on.

- Building scalable backend API apps (autoscale based on seasonality) without requiring the upfront provisioning of resources

- Workflows with no-code message processing steps requiring on-demand execution and scaling

The list of use cases provided here covers the most frequently used examples. If your API requirements fall in one of these categories, then you must contemplate using serverless technologies.

Although it is not mandatory to always use serverless technologies, cloud providers are continuously making investments in this area to bring in new features and capabilities. Hence, it will be worthwhile for the development teams to start accessing the use cases and get orientated with the approach. In the following sections, we will explore how API-led architectures can be implemented in Azure using the Azure services available.

Implementing API-led architectures in Azure

The reference architecture provided is based on the services that are in **General Availability** (**GA**) at the time of writing this book. Please continue to check the Azure architecture center for any latest updates or new services released by Microsoft.

Reference architecture for an enterprise API platform

Enterprise API platforms are typically very robust in nature, spanning from just a few services to hundreds of microservices, each solving a specific business problem. Moreover, there will be different types of APIs (internal, external, and public), making the hosting demands quite complex while addressing security and other usage-related requirements.

There is a wide variety of choices available to teams when building solutions for the Azure cloud. A very high-level sample representative reference architecture for building an API-centric solution is depicted in *Figure 3.7*:

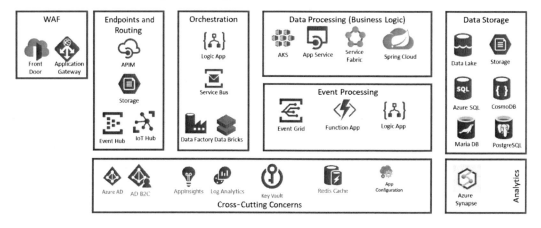

Figure 3.7 – Building blocks of an API-centric solution

As you would observe from the graphic, many Azure services are involved in building a proper end-to-end solution. Each service is a building block of the architecture. Depending on the nature of the API service or flows being implemented, multiple services can be stitched together to create the solution.

> **Note**
>
> The preceding reference architecture is meant to provide a big-picture view of the capabilities in the Azure cloud. It is not meant to be a comprehensive or exhaustive list of services that can be used in your scenario. Please visit the Azure Architecture Center for a more detailed understanding of workload-based reference architectures.

Read more on reference architectures here: https://docs.microsoft.com/ en-us/azure/architecture/. The important Azure services that are frequently used are briefly described in the following sections.

Azure services for hosting API solutions

API solutions typically make use of *compute plane* technologies to host and execute the associated transaction logic. Azure offers a variety of services for this purpose. The salient high-level features of the different Azure services that are frequently used in API-led architectures are mentioned in the following sections.

> **Note**
>
> In this section, only a high-level description is provided to introduce the Azure service. For more detailed information on each service, please refer to the detailed link provided for the corresponding service.

App Service

A fully managed compute platform for hosting API and web applications:

- Rapidly build, deploy, and manage powerful web and mobile multi-channel apps for employees or customers using a single backend.

- Quickly and easily scale globally on infrastructure you can trust.

- Enterprise-grade security and management, including AD authentication.

- Use your existing skills to code in your favorite language, framework, and IDE to build APIs and apps faster than ever before.

- Use modern DevOps practices, continuous deployment, cloud debugging tools, and testing in production to streamline your development process.

- Integrate with API Management, Logic Apps, and many other Azure services.

Find out more on Azure App Service at the following link: `https://azure.microsoft.com/en-in/services/app-service/`.

Function App

A serverless compute platform for processing events with elastic scale:

- Expedite your development cycles by building granular code blocks or functions quickly.

- The service can scale on demand and charges will be based on consumption. A fixed pricing plan is also available for very high usage scenarios.

Find out more on Azure Functions at the following link: `https://azure.microsoft.com/en-in/services/functions/`.

Logic App

A cloud-based integration service that is used for the execution of no-code workflows:

- Offers a designer view to model your business processes and workflows visually.

- Build a no-code HTTP REST API for use in web, mobile, and API apps.

- Automate EAI, B2B, and business processes using integration accounts.

- Connect to on-premises data through connectors and data gateways.

- Offer a variety of invocation options such as HTTP triggers, event-based triggers, or even a scheduled trigger.

Find out more on the Logic App service at the following link: `https://azure.microsoft.com/en-in/services/logic-apps/`.

Azure Kubernetes Service (AKS)

Microsoft's version of the open source Kubernetes cluster implementation. It makes it easy to build and operate the Kubernetes cluster by offloading complex Kubernetes creation and management tasks to Microsoft Azure, such as the controller and scheduler.

A Kubernetes cluster consists of the following:

- A node pool comprising nodes that can be scaled up based on demand.

- Pods that run application workloads using containers within the nodes.

- Cluster master nodes provide the core Kubernetes services and orchestration of application workloads.

Kubernetes has evolved to become the leader among container orchestration engines and is widely used in the industry to build high-scale reliable services.

Find out more on Azure Kubernetes Service at the following link: `https://azure.microsoft.com/en-in/services/kubernetes-service/`.

Service Fabric

Azure Service Fabric is Microsoft's distributed systems platform for running highly scalable and reliable microservices. It provides an SDK that makes it easy to package, deploy, and manage microservices and containers. It is used to run many of the services in Azure and components in Windows Server 2016 and higher versions.

All services deployed within the Service Fabric cluster must be developed using the Service Fabric programming model. The key differentiator of Service Fabric is its strong focus on running stateful services.

Find out more on Azure Service Fabric at the following link: `https://azure.microsoft.com/en-us/services/service-fabric/`.

Azure Sprint Cloud

Azure Spring Cloud is a fully managed service in Azure that is suitable for running your Sprint Boot microservices without any code changes to the applications. Azure Spring Cloud was originally designed to support Java Spring Boot applications and has been enhanced to include support for ASP.NET Core Steeltoe applications as well.

Azure Sprint cloud provides comprehensive tooling support for your API life cycle management.

Discover more on Azure Spring Cloud at the following link: `https://azure.microsoft.com/en-us/services/spring-cloud/`.

Additional services for building end-to-end solutions

The following list of additional services is typically required for building end-to-end solutions.

Azure Active Directory/Azure AD B2C

A cloud-based identity management solution from Microsoft, able to manage both external and internal user identities. Azure AD B2C (short for Business to Customer) is an extension of the Azure AD and preferably used when the application is required to manage external customer or partner identities for access and authorization.

Read more on Azure AD and AAD B2C at the following link: `https://azure.microsoft.com/en-us/services/active-directory/external-identities/b2c/`.

API Management

Azure API Management provides a governance layer on top of all published APIs. This service is covered in more detail in *Chapter 10, APIs as a Monetized Product*.

Read more about Azure API Management at the following link: `https://docs.microsoft.com/en-us/azure/api-management/api-management-key-concepts`.

Application Gateway

This serves as a **Web Application Firewall (WAF)** component to check various types of security rules while processing a request.

Key features of Application Gateway include the following:

- WAF
- Connection draining
- URL-based routing
- Redirection
- Cookie-based session affinity
- SSL termination
- Custom error pages
- Multi-site homing
- Re-writing HTTP headers
- WebSocket and HTTP/2 traffic

Read more about Azure Application Gateway at the following link: `https://docs.microsoft.com/en-us/azure/application-gateway/overview`.

Azure Front Door

This is Microsoft's latest offering for providing a layer of security on top of your web or API applications. It uses the backbone network of Azure to offer low-latency access to other PaaS resources. It is like Application Gateway from a WAF perspective, but it operates at Layer 7 (HTTP/HTTPS).

Read more on Azure Front Door at the following link: `https://docs.microsoft.com/en-us/azure/frontdoor/front-door-overview`.

Service Bus

A highly scalable and reliable messaging service from Microsoft. It supports three different types of communication options:

- Queues
- Topics (and subscriptions)
- Relay

It is widely used in various brokered messaging scenarios.

Read more at the following link: `https://azure.microsoft.com/en-in/services/service-bus/`.

Event Hub

A highly scalable event ingestion service capable of processing millions of events per second. This is typically used as a big data streaming service. It supports a partitioning strategy by consumers and allows for further scaling and separation of the streaming data.

Read more about Azure Event Hub at the following link: `https://docs.microsoft.com/en-us/azure/event-hubs/event-hubs-about`.

IoT Hub

IoT Hub was designed to be a bidirectional messaging service, allowing for the streaming of telemetry events generated by the devices at a great scale, while also allowing for cloud-to-device communications. For most of the event messaging scenarios, Event Hub should suffice. However, if your situation has **cloud to device (C2D)** and **device to cloud (D2C)** scenarios, then an IoT hub is the preferred choice of service.

Read more about Azure IoT Hub at the following link: `https://docs.microsoft.com/en-us/azure/iot-hub/about-iot-hub`.

Event Grid

Event Grid is a fully managed service that allows for seamless integration across various applications and Azure services using the event messaging pattern. This service is widely used for building event-driven serverless applications in Azure.

Read more about Event Grid at the following link: `https://docs.microsoft.com/en-us/azure/event-grid/overview`.

Application Insights

An Azure Monitor feature that monitors live applications in Azure and diagnoses issues or exceptions in web services through the capture of log traces. This service also gives insights into various health-related KPIs of a service, such as response times, failure rates, and usage.

Read more about Application Insights at the following link: `https://docs.microsoft.com/en-us/azure/azure-monitor/app/app-insights-overview`.

Azure Storage services

Azure Storage is a highly scalable, secure, durable, and reliable cloud storage solution. It is widely used while building applications and is generally utilized for low-cost, long-term storage requirements.

Read more about Azure Storage services at the following link: `https://docs.microsoft.com/en-us/azure/storage/`.

Case study elaboration – Packt Insurance Inc.

For any enterprise context, API platforms are built using microservices. Hence, these services can be implemented using one or more API styles that may be relevant depending on the nature of the business and technical requirements.

In the following sections, we will expand on the case study scenario by applying the concepts presented in this chapter. We will investigate the various API styles that will be useful for implementing the different microservices. We will also attempt to map some of the Azure services to create a very basic and high-level architectural blueprint. The sole objective is for you to understand what steps must be taken to identify architecture decisions and make a record of them.

API style fitment analysis

From the previous sections, it is evident that an enterprise API platform will comprise multiple API styles. You must pick the style that best suits the purpose. While certain styles may be preferred in general, considering that a wide range of use cases and integration points have to be accommodated, you will definitely need to try out different API styles.

For the Packt Insurance Inc. scenario, let's analyze which API styles will be useful to meet the technical requirements of the APIs:

API Architecture Style	Fitment Analysis
RPC + XML / JSON	This style will be preferred for submitting quote requests that have to operate in a request/response fashion. Typically, the broker will submit the details and will expect a quote to be returned as the response containing all the information that has to be shared with the customer.
REST + JSON	This style will be used for building APIs that perform CRUD operations on the underlying data store entities.
GraphQL	This style will be utilized for the execution of complex queries on the various entity objects. It is typically required by backend applications to support various query patterns to suit the needs of the administrator.
Event-Driven / Async Messaging	This style can be used for all fire-and-forget submission requests, such as filling in claims or even signing up for a policy. The processing of the data happens through an offline process, and updates can be shared periodically with the customer through notification alerts.
Hypermedia	For the context scenario, there will be limited use of this API style. The use of this style is largely dependent on the design of the user experience for mobile or web apps. Hence, for the purpose of this case study analysis, this style will not be considered further.

Microservices and API styles

A microservice can comprise one or more APIs. Hence, you may have to build different types of APIs to meet the purpose of the API.

In the following section, let's identify the various styles that will be used to build the various microservices for the Packt Insurance API platform:

Microservice APIs	RPC (JSON / XML)	REST + JSON	Event Messaging	GraphQL
Customers		X		
Quotes	X	X		X
Rules and Risks	X			
Policies		X	X	X
Claims		X	X	X
Payments		X	X	X

API platform architecture

Building upon the concepts presented in the preceding sections, let's identify the various Azure resources that can be leveraged for the Packt Insurance solution. The idea here is to provide a view on how to group the various technical capabilities into a logical view that can be expanded and tailored based on the needs of your project.

A very high-level solution architecture for the Packt Insurance Inc. API platform is provided here:

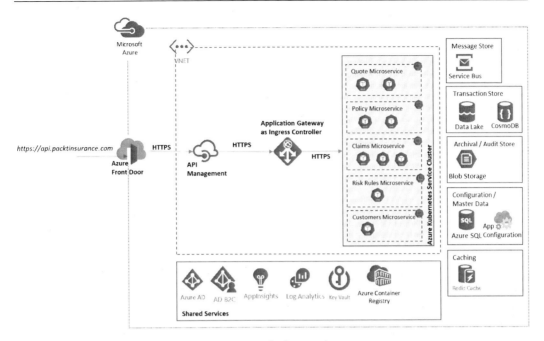

Figure 3.8 – API platform architecture

For this case study, we have selected Azure Kubernetes Services as the microservices platform as it offers a wide variety of benefits for a complex enterprise-scale application. However, variations of this architecture are also possible using the other technologies that are listed earlier in the reference architecture.

The preceding solution architecture depicted is meant to serve as a guide only, and certain solution concern areas, such as multi-tenancy (deployment isolation by region) and high availability and disaster recovery strategies have not been factored in. These topics are covered in subsequent chapters and the solution implementation patterns are explained.

Summary

In this chapter, we have reviewed some of the most important architecture principles and the impact they may have on the architecture and design of an API. We have also done a comparative study of the various API styles and analyzed what to choose depending on the business context and requirements.

Developers can build an API platform using one or more styles in the Azure cloud. There are a lot of options when it comes to hosting API solutions. Each has its own unique advantage. With serverless architectures, organizations can deploy API solutions really quickly and start realizing the business benefits.

In the next chapter, we will focus on understanding how to ensure the quality of your API service or product, how to measure them, and what tactical plans must be created to achieve this.

Additional reading

- Open Group – Architecture Principles: `https://pubs.opengroup.org/architecture/togaf8-doc/arch/chap29.html`

- Serverless computing and applications on Microsoft Azure: `https://azure.microsoft.com/en-in/overview/serverless-computing/`

- Azure Architecture Center: `https://docs.microsoft.com/en-us/azure/architecture/`

- Azure Compute Options Decision Tree: `https://docs.microsoft.com/en-us/azure/architecture/guide/technology-choices/compute-decision-tree`

- Azure Messaging Choice: `https://docs.microsoft.com/en-us/azure/architecture/guide/technology-choices/messaging`

4
Assuring the Quality of the API Service (or Product)

All software engineering teams strive to create a quality product as an output from the weeks of planning, designing, developing, and testing cycles. This, however, is not possible unless there is a clear and common understanding of the quality goals (or attributes) of the product under development.

A product backlog in the form of **architecture backlog stories** must be created and prioritized in a timely fashion to accomplish the targets/metrics set for these quality attributes. Otherwise, late discovery of critical issues, and subsequent fixing at a later stage in the project lifecycle, will turn out to be very costly.

The purpose of this chapter is to understand the important quality attributes that will apply to API-centric solutions. The objective is to assess the impact of non-functional requirements on the solution design and what trade-offs are necessary to achieve a highly reliable API platform.

By the end of this chapter, you will understand the importance of creating an architectural backlog to track solution-critical quality requirements, define and measure them, and what trade-offs to apply for the given business context.

In this chapter, we are going to cover the following main topics:

- The ISO 25010 standard for software quality

- The **Architecture Tradeoff Analysis Method (ATAM)**

- The Azure Well-Architected Framework

- API security considerations

- Reliability through scale, performance, and availability

- Modeling performance based on scale requirements

- High-availability patterns

- Architecting for operations

- Understanding maintainability

- Tracking objectives using a quality dashboard

- Case study elaboration – Packt Insurance Inc.

> **Food for thought**
> Measure what matters – explore how you can make use of the **Objectives and Key Results (OKR)** framework to capture your architecture-critical nonfunctional requirements.

The ISO 25010 standard for software product quality

ISO (International Standards Organization) 25010:2011 defines the **Systems and software Quality Requirements and Evaluation (SQuaRE)** that applies to software engineering. The standard covers two models: a **Quality in Use** model, and a **Product Quality** model. This section primarily focuses on the latter model as it applies to the design of API-led solution architectures.

So, what is a **quality attribute**? In simple terms, it can be viewed as a goal or a requirement that a system must achieve for its acceptance by the various stakeholders and users of the system.

> **The quality in use model**
>
> The quality in use model is more appropriate to consider when building UI applications. It is very important for an overall end-to-end solution, as it focuses on user-centric attributes such as effectiveness, efficiency, satisfaction, safety, and context comprehensiveness. There is some degree of correlation with the product quality model. However, for the purpose of this book, we have excluded it from the discussion in this chapter.

The ISO 25010: 2011 definition (which superseded the existing ISO/IEC 9126 on software product quality) broadly classified the important characteristics or quality goals of the system into eight categories, depicted as follows.

Figure 4.1 – Software Product Quality characteristics as per the ISO 25010:2011 standard

These eight characteristics of product quality and their respective subqualities are described in the following sections. The definitions have been made contextual to API-centric solutions for you to understand the concepts easily and how you may correlate them to your API designs.

Functional Suitability

Functional Suitability represents the degree to which an API meets the defined business requirements both from a user and system perspective.

This characteristic is composed of the following three sub-characteristics:

- **Functional completeness**: The degree to which the set of operations and functions supported by the API covers all the intended tasks and user objectives

- **Functional correctness**: The degree to which the API provides the correct response output for a set of input parameters

- **Functional appropriateness**: The degree to which the set of operations and functions supported by the API can easily accomplish the specified tasks and objectives

Guidance for the development team

Functional Suitability focuses primarily on the coverage of the business requirements, and whether all the specifications that are part of the scope have been implemented or not. Hence, you can adopt the following recommended strategies to measure this:

- Implement a requirement traceability matrix, by breaking down the requirements into a well-organized product backlog and then subsequently detailing out the stories and then capturing the implementation tasks, test cases, and any test reports.

- Ensure that there is a test case for each specific scenario, including both happy paths and exception flows. Ensure that the pass percentage of such test cases is greater than 95%.

- Analyze usage statistics of the API and observe whether the conversion rate is high.

Operability/Usability

Operability(Usability) is the degree to which an API can be used by the intended consumers to achieve the specified goals with greater satisfaction within the specified context of use.

This characteristic is composed of the following six sub-characteristics:

- **Appropriateness recognizability**: The degree to which API consumers can recognize whether it is appropriate for their needs.

- **Learnability**: The degree to which API consumers can easily understand how to use and invoke the API operations.

- **Operability**: The degree to which the API consumers can connect and use the API.

- **User error protection**: The degree to which the API implements validations to prevent data loss due to end user errors.

- **User interface aesthetics**: This characteristic *does not apply* to API products.

  Some tips on UI aesthetics can be referenced here: `https://medium.com/nyc-design/7-rules-for-creating-visually-aesthetic-ui-6ac0fe8856f`.

- **Accessibility**: This characteristic *does not apply* to API products.

  As a reference, you can refer to this guide: `https://www.w3.org/WAI/fundamentals/accessibility-intro/`.

Guidance for the development team

Operability measures revolve around the production use of the API platform, and how easy it is for external developers or partners to integrate their applications with the public API interfaces. Hence, you can adopt the following recommended strategies to achieve this:

- Implement an API discovery and documentation portal that can be leveraged by the developer community at the time of integration.

- Provide readily usable samples demonstrating how the API accomplishes the various business operations.

- Make use of standardized API styles and connectivity approaches to avoid requiring any learning curves.

- Implement data validation as part of the interfaces to avoid registering junk or invalid data.

Reliability

Reliability is the degree to which an API can serve its consumers consistently over a specified period of time.

This characteristic is composed of the following four sub-characteristics:

- **Maturity**: The degree to which the API meets the need for reliability under normal operation

- **Availability**: The degree to which the API is operational and accessible when required for use

- **Fault tolerance**: The degree to which the API is operational, overcoming any intermittent hardware outages or faults
- **Recoverability**: The degree to which, in the event of an interruption or a failure, the API can recover automatically to a healthy state

Guidance for the development team

Reliability focuses on ensuring that the API is available to its intended users without any interruption as per their desired usage. Hence, you can adopt the following recommended strategies to achieve this:

- Define availability requirements and understand downtime implications.
- Avoid single points of failure through redundancy.
- Prevent data loss or corruption through geo-replication or event-based patterns.
- Implement automation to periodically scan and detect failures.
- Implement automatic failover strategies to reduce downtime.

Performance Efficiency

Performance Efficiency represents the overall health and performance of an API under impact from increased loads or seasonality.

This characteristic is composed of the following sub-characteristics:

- **Time behavior**: The degree to which the API response and processing times and throughput rates meet the acceptable thresholds defined for the operations
- **Resource utilization**: The degree to which the API makes use of the available system resources (namely, CPU, memory, IOPs, and so on) when performing under an increased load
- **Capacity**: The degree to which the API can meet the maximum limits, as defined by **requests per second** (**RPS**) without significantly impacting other factors

Guidance for the development team

The Performance Efficiency characteristic attempts to ensure that users are happy with their experience of the API platform, and any frontend applications that integrate with the API achieve a good responsive UI. Hence, you can adopt the following recommended strategies to achieve this:

- Architect for scale, identify scaling requirements diligently.
- Conduct design and code reviews to identify performance bottlenecks.
- **Left shift performance testing**, making it part of your unit testing.
- Establish DevOps practices to detect and alert on performance issues.
- Incorporate robust telemetry and logging to measure and monitor the performance of your API and its internal components.

Security

Security is the degree to which the API protects information and data so that consumers can access the operations and underlying data as per their authorization levels only.

This characteristic is composed of the following sub-characteristics:

- **Confidentiality**: The degree to which the API ensures that data is accessible only to authorized users
- **Integrity**: The degree to which the API prevents unauthorized access
- **Non-repudiation**: The degree to which the API ensures that only verified transactions are permitted by it
- **Accountability**: The degree to which the API tracks the actions performed on an entity
- **Authenticity**: The degree to which the API can verify the credentials of the consumer

Guidance for the development team

Security deals with the overall defense-in-depth principles, attempting to secure all layers of the solution, which include infrastructure, individual resources, access paths, and even the data. You can adopt the following recommended strategies to achieve this:

- Establish a security culture – conduct training for the team.

- Establish a centralized team of security champions who will dedicatedly investigate the various security aspects.

- Ensure that best practices are followed by the book, and any deviations are real exceptions only.

- Make use of available static analyzers or tools, to scan and detect vulnerabilities in any code.

- Conduct security testing wherever possible, including penetration testing to prevent any security breaches or mistakes in code.

Compatibility

Next, **Compatibility** is the degree to which the API interfaces can be consumed and integrated easily with other systems or applications without impacting any existing solutions.

This characteristic is composed of the following sub-characteristics:

- **Co-existence**: The degree to which the API can support newer versions of the product without impacting any existing applications or integrations

- **Interoperability**: The degree to which the API can support the exchange of information with other systems

Guidance for the development team

Compatibility is an important attribute that allows the API to be easily used by other platforms or solutions, making integrations easier. You can adopt the following recommended strategies as a team to achieve this:

- Make use of API versioning on both data and interface contracts.

- Design for backward compatibility.

- Make use of industry standards (for example, JSON API and OpenAPI specifications) while implementing and publishing the API endpoints.

Maintainability

This characteristic represents the degree of ease with which the code and logic of the API can be modified and deployed to production without much overhead or cycle time.

This characteristic is composed of the following sub-characteristics:

- **Modularity**: The degree to which the API can be broken into discrete components such that a change to one component does not have any significant impact on other components

- **Reusability**: The degree to which the API operations and the underlying implementation can be easily reused across other API products

- **Analyzability**: The degree to which the impact of any issues can be easily identified by the API

- **Modifiability**: The degree to which the API can be easily extended without affecting the quality of the solution

- **Testability**: The degree to which the test conditions for an API can be easily created and implemented

Guidance for the development team

Maintainability focuses on making the API easily modifiable without incurring maintenance costs or regression defects, both of which are costly. Hence, the team can adopt the following recommended strategies to achieve this:

- Make use of static code analyzers to measure code quality.

- Foster code reuse, and make use of **Dependency Injection** or similar strategies.

- Conduct manual code inspections to detect design constraints.

- Fully automate API testing.

- Left shift functional testing, detecting issues through build breaks.

Portability

Portability is the degree of effectiveness and efficiency with which the API solution can be transferred from one platform to another or one environment to another.

This characteristic is composed of the following sub-characteristics:

- **Adaptability**: The degree to which the API product can adapt to the provisioned hardware or software systems
- **Installability** The degree to which the API can be easily deployed or uninstalled
- **Replaceability** The degree to which the API can easily be upgraded to a newer version

Guidance for the development team

Portability attempts to make the API platform easily deployable across multiple environments without requiring any modifications or significant effort. Hence, the team can adopt the following recommended strategies to achieve this:

- Achieve 100% automation of deployment procedures.
- Conduct deployment testing to ensure the sanctity of the deployment scripts.

So, how do you *measure the quality* of any API product? Considering what we have discussed in the previous sections, it is evident that for some of the attributes, it will be **analytical** as you will have quantitative data to substantiate it, whereas, for many others, it is more of a **qualitative** aspect that must be defined through some sort of conditions of satisfaction that are agreed based on consultation with key stakeholders.

Hence, it is imperative that a good amount of focus is given to the quality attributes during the initial phases of the development lifecycle. That's the only way quality-related risks can be identified and mitigated to the satisfaction of all.

> **Track quality attributes in your Product backlog**
>
> As per your organization's internal IT standards, you may use only a subset of the afore-listed quality attributes. The objective should be to identify clear business goals or metrics that are applicable to solution quality and then track them consistently to ensure compliance. In the absence of a tracking mechanism, it will be difficult to certify the quality of your API product.

In the next section, we will take a brief look into the **Architecture Tradeoff Analysis Method (ATAM)**, from the **Software Engineering Institute (SEI)**. The goal of ATAM is risk reduction and better architecture decisions revolving around quality attributes.

Architecture Tradeoff Analysis Method (ATAM)

Simply put, the ATAM process is a technique that can be used to find the right tuning of the various quality attributes to achieve the optimal quality for the given context.

You can read more about the ATAM process at `https://resources.sei.cmu.edu/library/asset-view.cfm?assetid=5177`.

The outputs of the ATAM review process are the following:

- An advisory, a recommendation, or a waiver for the target architecture based on the prioritized list of quality attributes
- Identification of the architecture risks that may have a high impact
- A record of the key architecture decisions in support of the suggested solution approach

Thus, we find that ATAM is a crucial and critical activity that must be carried out while defining the architecture of even API platforms. It is important to note that architecture can evolve or change over a period and having a record of the decisions will give a better perspective to the teams on what alternatives were considered and what was the basis of selecting one approach.

In the next section, we will review the principles of the Azure Well-Architected Framework, which provides good guidance around some of the aforementioned ISO standards to ensure a quality API service on the Azure cloud.

The Azure Well-Architected Framework

Around July 2020, Microsoft launched the **Well-Architected Framework** (**WAF**) for Azure. The WAF is a collection of industry-relevant best practices that are divided into five pillars:

- Cost management
- Operational excellence
- Performance efficiency
- Reliability
- Security

The WAF provides excellent prescriptive guidance that enables architects and developers to incorporate architecture best practices into their solutions.

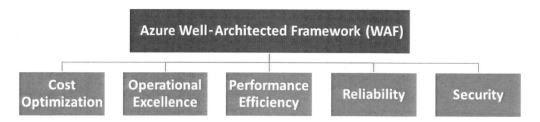

Figure 4.2 – Five pillars of the Azure Well-Architected Framework

Read more on the Azure WAF at `https://docs.microsoft.com/en-us/azure/architecture/framework/`.

You should consider the WAF guidance for building high-quality API platforms in Azure. The guidance covers the most important quality attributes that play a significant role in all your cloud investments.

Let's now review some of the benefits of using WAF in your solutions.

Benefits of using WAF

The key benefits of using the WAF recommended practices while designing and implementing your API-centric solutions are as follows:

- **Lower Total Cost of Ownership (TCO):**

  This is critical for start-ups and small businesses where IT budgets are a constraint. By making use of Azure resources that offer a consumption-based pricing model, they can easily achieve cost optimization through a *pay-per-use* model.

  Large businesses can also optimize their cloud usage costs by leveraging the various consumption-related metrics and reports available out of the box in the *Azure Cost Management and Billing* section. You can analyze these reports to either remove unused resources or optimize the pricing tier of various resources.

- **Identified and mitigated (security) risks:**

  All businesses operate with a certain degree of risk. The more effective they are in mitigating the risks, the less disruption and revenue loss they incur. By following the WAF practices, organizations can proactively assess risks so that they can be preempted easily.

- **Release agility**:

  The cycle time of releasing new services has shrunk significantly. If you are a digital business, you must look at expediting releases to be competitive. The WAF guidance is primarily targeted at improving your ability to deploy stuff to production faster than you might be used to doing.

- **Businesses allowed to run 24x7**:

  The availability of a service when they need it makes customers hooked onto any platform or application. Hence, most businesses are shifting toward a 24x7 model with high reliability.

- **Industry best practices for cloud apps used**:

  The WAF guidance incorporates learnings from numerous customers using the Azure cloud. Hence, the best practices list it has is based on what they have experienced while running their line-of-business and mission-critical applications on the Azure cloud.

- **Maximized end customer experience**:

  The success of any application depends on how well it is adopted by the partners and the customers, and how easily they can use it to realize their business benefits. Running ML loops on the feedback captured can help improve the engagement index immensely.

WAF recommended practices

The following are a few of the important recommended practices of the WAF:

WAF Pillar	Recommended Practices
Cost Optimization	• Plan and estimate costs. • Provision with optimization, scale as appropriate. • Use monitoring and analytics to gain cost insights. • Maximize the efficiency of the cloud spend by eliminating wastage (through resource deletion/shutdown when not in use).
Operational Excellence	• Leverage the power of DevOps – design, build, and orchestrate with modern practices. • Logging – the more the merrier: use monitoring and analytics to gain operational insights. • Use automation to reduce manual effort and error. • Automated testing – try reliability.
Performance Efficiency	• Define scalability needs. • Conduct performance modeling. • Make use of architecture/design patterns that support scale-out. • Plan for autoscaling. • Measure and monitor performance. • Identify and fix bottlenecks. • Optimize network and storage performance. • Avoid geo-distributed latencies.
Reliability	• High availability – design for failure and fault tolerance. • Disaster recovery – conduct risk assessment and process inventory. • Incorporate "self-healing" techniques. • Plan for testing reliability (must have >= 99.99%).
Security	• Defense in depth (both in infrastructure and code). • Plan security training for your team. • Conduct threat modeling. • **Secure Development Lifecycle (SDL)** – Review, understand, and follow best practices.

As you start using the WAF for your Azure cloud solutions, you must clearly identify the business goals that are relevant for your business context across the five pillars. You can begin by taking an assessment to measure the current state and then review the recommendations to define a roadmap of improvement initiatives.

In the subsequent sections, we will review, in detail, some of the most important quality requirements and how they may have an impact on your API-led architectures.

API security considerations

Information security and preventing unauthorized access is the most important focus area for all API platforms. Attackers are always on the lookout to exploit any vulnerabilities and over the course of time, cyber threats have increased tremendously. Teams have been busy detecting these threats and then subsequently establishing practices and solutions that mitigate the security risks.

Security is one of the most important aspects of any API-led architecture. Enterprises must ensure that no data breaches happen as it may have drastic consequences for the business.

Let's look at some of the core principles of the Security Frame concept, which can be easily applied to API-led architectures.

Core principles – the Security Frame analysis

The following categories of security considerations, referred to as **Security Frame** in the diagram, explain the core security principles that must be followed in the design of an API solution:

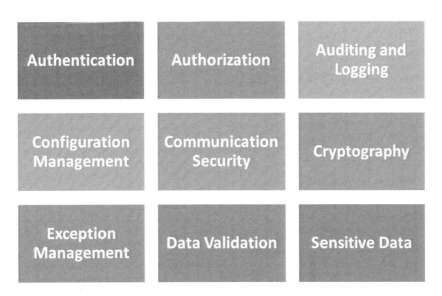

Figure 4.3 – Security Frame

While Security Frame is a good framework for your security design considerations, it is not meant to be an exhaustive list of controls that can be implemented. Security guidelines are ever-evolving as newer threats are identified. Hence, it is recommended that API development teams constantly review, evaluate, and revise the security controls applied.

> **Note**
> The subsequent sections are meant to serve only as basic guidance. Development teams must do a thorough analysis of their project context to capture important security requirements, and then plan appropriate controls to mitigate all security risks. As a rule of thumb, for any software system, security takes precedence over all other requirements.

Authentication

Authentication is the process of proving identity through various means, such as username and password, certificates, tokens, keys, and so on. This is an important property to ensure that resources are accessible only to genuine parties.

Most enterprise applications need to interact with a wide range of applications, sometimes even legacy applications that are deployed in on-premises data centers, others being SaaS and cloud-native applications. Therefore, a wide variety of authentication schemes may have to be supported.

The following are some of the general authentication schemes that are typically used by any API platform:

- **SAML tokens**: For applications that rely on federated identity based on SAML 2.0 protocol
- **Bearer tokens**: For modern applications that rely on Azure Active Directory (or Azure AD B2C) and similar identity stores, which support **OpenID Connect (OIDC)** and OAuth v2 protocols
- **Client certificates**: For applications that are exposed to third parties and want stronger security assurances, such as revocation, rotation, and so on

Authorization

Authorization is about how the application provides access controls for roles, resources, and operations. The principle of least privileges is kept in mind while granting access to any role, resource, or operation.

The following are some of the areas where authorization is keenly analyzed:

- Access to resources on an Azure subscription
- Access to file shares
- Access to data stores such as SQL, Azure Storage, and so on
- Access to keys/secrets that are stored in Azure Key Vault

- Service accounts under which applications run and so on

- API-specific **Role-Based Access Control (RBAC)** or **Attribute-Based Access Control (ABAC)**

> **Attribute-Based Access Control (ABAC)**
>
> Attribute-Based Access Control, also known as policy- or business rules-driven access control, is an approach that grants or denies access to an API operation depending on the attributes of the user or the resource and associated data. This is quite a flexible model of controlling access as the rules or policies can be contextualized to the attributes of the assigned user, resource, environment, and so on. You can read more about it here: `https://www.sciencedirect.com/topics/computer-science/attribute-based-access-control`

Auditing and Logging

Auditing and Logging, in the context of security requirements, refers to how security-related events are recorded, monitored, and audited.

For an API platform, all events such as sign-in activities, API access and errors, sensitive operations, and so on must be audited and logged. Further, it must also be ensured that sensitive information will not be stored in logs. Only non-sensitive identifiers such as `Event Id` and `User Id`, which are needed to trace back an operation, must be logged.

> **GDPR**
>
> You must evaluate your logging approach against any GDPR-specific policies that may apply to your specific context. For data belonging to users who are residents of European Union countries, additional anonymization and data pseudonymization techniques may have to be considered before anything gets saved as part of the logs.

Configuration management

Configuration management is about handling security-related configurations to minimize the security attack surface and enable certain best practices.

Some examples are the following:

- Configuring database connection strings or access keys

- Configuring security policies such as CORS for APIs

- Configuring service throttling limits wherever applicable

- Configuring out-of-the-box features such as transparent data encryption for databases, or cache-related settings

---

Make use of Infrastructure as a Code

For Azure resources, it is recommended that configurations be made consistent using ARM templates, policies, and/or PowerShell scripts wherever applicable.

Communication security

Communication security is about the secure transmission of data over the wire. It includes transport-level security to message-level security.

The following are some of the considerations:

- All interactions with the API platform must happen over a secure channel. This ensures that data in transit is always secure.

- In scenarios where message-level security is explicitly required, if the platform provides **out-of-the-box (OOTB)** security capabilities, for example, **AS2 message encryption**, the OOTB configurations must be leveraged. For AS2 messages, asymmetric encryption is supported, and the certificates can be configured in the **integration accounts**.

- In scenarios where OOTB message-level security is not available, you must plan for attaining the confidentiality of messages that are exchanged between the source and the destination. Additional encryption/decryption algorithms may have to be considered to process highly confidential messages.

Cryptography

Cryptography is about how the platform enforces confidentiality and integrity aspects. Some of the considerations in this aspect are the following:

- The use of strong and industry-standard cryptographic algorithms and key lengths

- Tamper-proofing of critical resources (for example, sensitive files, API parameters, and so on)

- Secret/key/certificate management (generation, rotation, revocation, and so on)

Exception management

Exception management refers to how applications handle errors and exceptions. It must be ensured that in the event of exceptions, the application will support graceful failover without revealing sensitive details via error messages. Moreover, the corresponding error information must be audited/logged so that suitable actions can be taken as required by the operations team based on the nature of the incident.

Data validation

Data validation refers to how the solution filters, scrubs, or rejects input before additional processing, or how it sanitizes the output (if required).

Input data validation must be prioritized and captured as part of the API requirements themselves. In the absence of any being available, the project teams must still implement validations on a best-effort basis to prevent any malicious use of the system.

Sensitive data

Sensitive data refers to how the solution handles any data that must be protected either in transit or at rest. API platforms use a variety of storage technologies for persisting their data.

Some of the considerations in this frame include the following:

- Ensuring data classification is done per application and sensitive data in each case is identified
- Ensuring controls such as **Transparent Data Encryption** (**TDE**) and column-level encryption are applied to data stores wherever applicable to ensure the confidentiality of the data
- Ensure that source code does not store sensitive data
- Ensure that all secrets are stored in highly secure **Hardware Security Module** (**HSM**)-backed stores such as Azure Key Vault or any other proprietary/third-party secret store
- Ensure that all data is encrypted before saving it in storage (encryption for data at rest)

> **Encryption at rest**
>
> In cases where persistent data storage must be used, the corresponding security controls must be analyzed to ensure the confidentiality of the data at rest. The implementation will comply with the guidelines for Azure Data Encryption at Rest, available at `https://docs.microsoft.com/en-us/azure/security/azure-security-encryption-atrest`.

In the next section, we will discuss the concept of Security Development Lifecycle processes that development teams must adopt to ensure that security practices are properly followed by teams.

The Security Development Lifecycle (SDL)

The **Security Development Lifecycle** (**SDL**) is a process that emphasizes the inclusion of additional security practices and activities as part of your standard software development lifecycle process to accomplish the security goals of your solution.

Microsoft pioneered the Security Development Lifecycle process as part of the Trustworthy Computing initiative around 2002. With the growth of the internet, various virus and malware attacks were witnessed on a large scale.

Hence, Microsoft realized that it was pivotal to start taking security-related concerns more seriously and bake them into all its products. Thus the initial version of the SDL process evolved, also popularly known as **Microsoft Security Development Lifecycle** (**MS SDL**). Since then, many other software companies have created their own version of the SDL based on the MS SDL process.

You can read more about MS SDL practices at `https://www.microsoft.com/en-us/securityengineering/sdl/practices`.

The following figure depicts the key SDL activities during various phases of the development lifecycle:

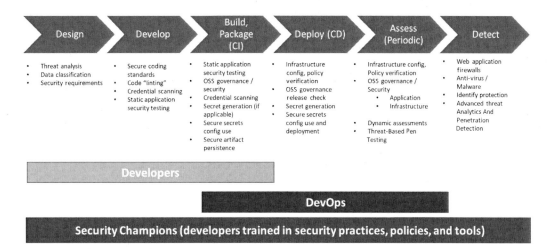

Figure 4.4 – Key activities of the SDL

The different stages in the SDL are briefly described as follows:

- **Design**: This is the very first phase, during which threat modeling is conducted for the proposed solution architecture and design. Security risks, if any, must be mitigated by capturing the controls that will be applied. Other activities involve a review of the security requirements for the project as well as the data classification requirements.

- **Develop**: During the **Develop** phase, the security-related **subject matter expert (SME)** will conduct code reviews using either manual inspection techniques or running static analyzers to detect any security issues in the code components being developed.

- **Build & Package** (**CI**): As part of the **Continuous Integration** (**CI**) process, static code analyzers and other security-related tools must be integrated within the verification builds. This prevents the leaking of security issues to the stable code branch, as the merge will not succeed if the build fails.

- **Deploy** (**CD**): The deployment scripts must also comply with the various security controls that must be in place for the infrastructure and solution components. This can be governed through the usage of cloud security-related policies and standards, which must apply consistently across all workloads.

- **Assess (Periodic)**: Once a stable version of the solution has been deployed, the SME should conduct periodic reviews to detect any deviations from the established practices.

- **Detect**: The operations team, as part of ongoing monitoring, must detect and respond to any security incidents in a timely fashion. A thorough post-mortem analysis must be done to prevent the recurrence of the same incidents.

The SDL focuses on eliminating the common mistakes that are repeated by the development teams. Security defect fixes can be very costly with a high impact. The SDL defines a set of standardized process steps mandating certain important security activities such as architecture analysis, code reviews, and penetration testing to provide some degree of assurance of the quality of the product being developed.

Reliability through scale, performance, availability

As discussed earlier, reliability can be broadly defined as the *probability that the system will function as per its expected behavior under the specified environmental conditions within a specified time.*

As you know from the previous chapters, API platforms are the backbone of the digital channels for an enterprise. Hence, ensuring the reliability of APIs is fundamental to the adoption and usage of digital experiences. In fact, this topic is so important that a complete engineering discipline, named **Site Reliability Engineering** (**SRE**), has emerged, and organizations are hiring professionals to tackle the complexity associated with it, to achieve appropriate levels of reliability for their digital services.

In the following sections, we will briefly touch upon the important topics related to SRE. For a more comprehensive study, please make use of the references listed in the *Further reading* section.

> **Note:**
> In this chapter, we will discuss reliability together with scalability, performance, and availability as these attributes are interlinked, and an impact in one area affects the others.

Site Reliability Engineering (SRE)

SRE is an engineering discipline that is devoted to enabling organizations to achieve appropriate levels of reliability for their software services and systems. SRE originated with Google in 2003 when Ben Treynor, now Treynor Sloss, after taking the leadership role for the production team, inculcated the thinking among software engineers to design systems from an operations point of view. Basically, the thinking was that software developers must focus on the end goal of the platform, which would be measured through uptime and other operational metrics.

The team came up with many best practices that served as a culture shift for the development teams. Over the years, many new practices and processes have evolved, and you will find many books written on the subject.

You can read about building a robust SRE strategy here: `https://docs.microsoft.com/en-us/learn/paths/az-400-develop-sre-strategy/`.

SRE and DevOps are better together

DevOps is often confused with being an enhanced version of SRE. However, it is important to note that SRE has a specific focus area, whereas DevOps is a much broader subject that tends toward a total cultural shift of the development team by focusing on various aspects of an end-to-end lifecycle.

While there is some overlap between the principles and practices, they must be still considered as separate streams. A DevOps engineer should collaborate with an SRE engineer to achieve the overall goals of the enterprise.

Some of the key benefits of using SRE and DevOps are the following:

- Better reporting on metrics leading to more stable solutions
- Identifying issues and challenges early in the lifecycle
- The modernization of operations through automation
- Continuous improvement through continuous feedback and learning
- A higher customer satisfaction index

Now, let's look at how you can ensure proper reliability.

How do you ensure appropriate reliability?

The **degree of reliability** required for any business context varies based on the solution being developed. For example, if your retail outlet store opens for 14 hours, then your usage of any software system may be limited to the business hours with peaks at certain times of the day. However, if you are an online business, then you may require greater reliability as customers may place their orders at different times of the day based on their convenience. That is precisely the reason SRE practices can be tailored to achieve the *appropriate level of reliability*.

Reliability is defined and measured using **Service-Level Objectives (SLOs)**. Simply put, SLOs define the target level of reliability that must be achieved by any service. The goal should be enough for service consumers to remain satisfied. The SLOs can evolve or change depending on the demands of the business. However, the service owners must constantly measure the SLOs to detect any issues and take corrective actions. SLOs are measured usually as a percentage achievement over a period.

Another important term to note is **Service-Level Indicator (SLI)**. This is the metric that is used to calculate SLOs. SLIs are based on insights derived from the data captured through the various signals received when the service is being consumed by the customer. Hence, an SLI is always measured from a customer's point of view.

SLOs and SLIs always go hand in hand and are usually defined in an iterative manner. SLOs are driven by the key business objectives, whereas SLIs are driven by what it is possible to measure while implementing the service.

When you are building an API service, the first step of the process is to define the SLO benchmarks that must be achieved by the API once it's commissioned for production use. This is followed by the identification of the various metrics (or SLIs) that must be monitored for the service.

> **Set realistic reliability goals**
>
> Having a reliability goal of 100% is unrealistic. It is practically impossible to achieve this despite having redundancy in hardware or automated health checks with failover and so on. Hence, it is typically measured in terms of 9s (nines) as 99%, 99.9%, 99.99%, and so on.
>
> It is important to conduct a benefit analysis when designing systems with high-reliability goals, as there will always be a cost angle involved. Unless the revenue generated justifies the operational expense, reliability goals must be scrutinized to keep them appropriate. Sometimes even having lower reliability goals such as 90% may be acceptable for the given business context.

In subsequent sections, we will look at some of the commonly used SLOs and SLIs for an API service.

Commonly used SLOs for an API service

Some of the commonly used SLO types for an API service are listed here:

- **Response Time Latency**

  Response Time Latency is the amount of time elapsed between when a request for an operation is made and when the invoker can make use of the returned result. Latency is typically expressed as multiple target values (in milliseconds) across separate percentiles.

Sample Objectives
Requests in the last 5 minutes are served in <; 300 ms @ 95th percentile
Requests in the last 5 minutes are served in <; 750 ms @ 99th percentile
Requests in the last 5 minutes are served in <; 2000 ms @ 99.99th percentile

- **Success Rate**

  Success Rate measures whether the service is performing as expected (that is, not returning errors for every request). It is measured as the number of successful events divided by the number of total events, typically expressed in 9s.

Sample Objectives
99.99% of requests in the last 5 minutes were successful

- **Capacity or Throughput**

  This is the number of throttling-based responses when capacity is/is not available.

Sample Objectives
99.999% of responses are not throttling responses in any 1-minute window

- **Availability**

  Availability measures the service's uptime, measured from the perspective of a customer trying to make use of the service, and is typically measured in 9s. Availability SLOs are similar to Success Rate SLOs but do not verify that the return results match what is expected of the requests, merely that return results are flowing to the user. As a result, Availability SLOs should have a higher number of 9s than a Success Rate SLO.

Sample Objectives
99.999% of read and write requests in the last 5 minutes were successful

- **Interruption Rate**

  Interruption Rate measures the exact count of a specific type of event on a specific type of resource (for example, the number of VM reboots). Most services should not make use of Interruption Rate SLOs because a specific count of events typically does not scale as the number of users of the service scales.

Sample Objectives
An Azure IaaS Virtual Machine experiences on average no more than 1 unplanned VM restart over 1 year

- **Data Latency (Freshness)**

  Data Latency can be expressed as data freshness, or how old the data can be and still be served to users. Patch age is a form of latency SLO.

Sample Objectives
99% of assets served are less than 24 hours old

Having reviewed the important SLOs that must be defined for your API services, you now will gain an understanding of the related SLIs and how to measure them.

Defining, implementing, and measuring SLI metrics for an API platform

SLI metrics indicate the degree to which a service is providing the good experience that it was designed for. Hence, it can be expressed in the form of a ratio of two numbers, the numerator being the number of good events and the denominator being the total number of events. For an API service, events refer to the application-specific metrics that are captured during execution either as telemetry data or processed information.

For API platforms, the following SLIs are very common:

SLI	Description
Availability	This measure indicates whether the request was serviced or not by the API.
Latency	This measure indicates the overall time it took for the API to process the incoming request, and subsequently respond back with a reply.
Throughput	This measure indicates how many requests were handled by the API.
Success Rate	This measure indicates how many times the API successfully handled the incoming requests.
Error Rate	This measure indicates how many errors were generated for all the requests that were handled by the API.
Freshness	This measure indicates how many times the user received the latest data for read operations on the API, despite the underlying data store being updated with a certain write latency.
Correctness	This measure indicates whether the API was able to successfully process the request and return a valid and correct response to the end user.

A few examples of SLIs are as follows:

- The number of HTTP requests that were completed successfully within 1000ms / total number of HTTP requests.

- The number of search results that returned any products published to the catalog within 3 seconds / total number of searches.

> **Note:**
> There may be additional SLIs that you can measure to improve the overall reliability of the platform.

Once the SLI metrics have been defined, you must start analyzing what events or telemetry data to capture to measure the respective SLIs. For example, to measure availability, you must capture events to indicate whether the API service successfully processed your request or not. For HTTP-based services, Success or Failure is defined through HTTP status codes. Hence, the API design and implementation must ensure that proper HTTP status codes are emitted by the service while processing any request. SLI metrics are an important input to the API implementation.

For cloud-based systems, some of the metrics are available out of the box using the diagnostic and monitoring support available for the resources. Depending on your specific SLI requirements, additional monitoring data must be captured to calculate the metrics.

Percentile distribution and period of measurement

The two factors that play an important role in the measurement of the SLIs are the following:

- **Percentile Distribution**: For some of the SLIs, it is a general practice to calculate them using a percentile distribution technique. This gives better results as there will always be outliers that can skew the numbers if, say, a mean or median distribution technique is used.

- **Period of Measurement**: The period of measurement while defining an SLO is also very important. There will be a load on the system only during specific periods, and the remainder of the time, the system will be idle. Hence, the period of measurement is an important consideration, so that the reliability of the service can be guaranteed when it is likely to be used.

  This window can be 5 minutes to 24 hours depending on how you would like to monitor and calculate the SLI metric. Choosing the time window of measurement is very important as it must be aligned with the end users' expectations. The service must be available when they need it.

For example, let's consider that we want to measure the latency of API requests and define 3 seconds as the threshold for optimal performance. Hence, if we sort the response times for different API requests over a measurement window of, say, 1 hour, we may encounter a few of the API requests taking longer than 3 seconds, whereas most of them respond within the threshold limit. This is the expected behavior of the system.

The percentile distribution is meant to exclude outliers that may be due to intermittent issues as there are always too many parameters to control for any request. Usually, if the service responds properly within, say, the 90th or the 95th percentile measurement, it will be considered as having met the SLO.

In the next section, we will understand in a little more detail how to apply the SLIs to calculate the SLOs for your API service.

Using SLIs to calculate the initial SLOs for your API service

Monitoring logs will get captured automatically once the API service has been deployed and is in use. Now, let's say we analyze the data for, say, 1 week, and observe the following facts:

- Total requests: 123,456

- Total successful requests: 123,204

- 90th percentile latency: 497 ms

- 95th percentile latency: 870 ms

- 99th percentile latency: 1024 ms

Hence, for the SLO types, we can do the calculations as follows:

- Availability = (123,204 / 123,456) – 99.8%

- Latency = 90% (approx.) of the requests were served within 500 ms

- Latency = 98% (approx.) of the requests were served within 1000 ms

Considering the numbers above, we can start seeing some trends around the SLOs.

Now, let's say that at the time of the planning phase, we defined an aspirational latency SLO target of *90% of the requests will be processed within 500 ms with a success rate of 99% over a period of 1 week.*

With the data available from the logs, we can easily identify whether the SLO target was met or not. You can apply the same approach to identify compliance with other SLOs.

What are Service-Level Agreements?

Service-Level Agreements (**SLAs**) are agreements between a service provider and the customer of the service that define the degree of adherence to the agreed SLOs. SLAs carry legal and commercial penalties if they are not met by the service provider.

Modeling performance based on scale requirements

For a software system, **performance** generally refers to the overall responsiveness of a system when executing an action within a specified time period, while **scalability** is the ability of the system to handle increased user loads without constraining the resources that may have an impact on the performance of the system.

A system is deemed as scalable if the underlying resources are made available dynamically to support the increase in load. **Cloud applications** must be designed for scale and the traffic volume is difficult to predict at times. There may be seasonal spikes impacting the scale requirements, especially in a multi-tenant kind of scenario, when the service may serve requests for multiple tenants.

So, it is a good practice to design applications in such a way that they can scale out automatically to meet the peaks in demand. Basically, the system should just scale up or down based on the load. Scalability concerns not just compute instances, but other elements such as data storage, messaging infrastructure, and more.

> **Horizontal versus vertical scaling**
>
> *Horizontal scaling* or scale out basically refers to the ability of the cloud service to spin out additional compute instances or nodes to improve the performance of the application when under increased load, whereas *vertical scaling* or scale up refers to the ability to add more resources such as CPU, memory, and so on to the same cloud service instance to handle the increased load. Horizontal scaling is preferred over vertical scaling for API microservices as it ensures more predictable performance.

Hence, all enterprise systems must be designed and implemented to provide the right user experience for the expected levels of load. Otherwise, the impact could be catastrophic and may drastically impact the bottom line of the organization.

A common mistake seen among developers is the fact they tend to think of performance very late in the development cycle. They focus too much on functional requirements and do not consider the performance implications of the proposed solution design. Issues or bottlenecks can surface due to a variety of reasons, from poor architecture and design, bad code, or inappropriate resource allocation to even deployment scaling issues. The earlier a risk or issue is identified, the better the mitigation plan will be.

Hence, it is important to note that ensuring application performance cannot be a one-time activity. Throughout the lifecycle stages, certain specific activities must happen to manage the overall performance of the solution and achieve the business objectives. With the adoption of Agile methodologies, managing application performance is more of an iterative process.

In the next section, we will understand how to apply a process-oriented technique to manage the performance of an application.

The API (or application) performance management lifecycle

The performance of an API must be managed from its inception, through its upgrades and extensions, to the point when it is deprecated or no longer in use. Hence, a robust governance process must be in place to ensure that performance issues are detected and fixed early before they cause any major outages impacting the business.

Let's look at the various stages that comprise the performance management lifecycle:

Figure 4.5 – API performance management lifecycle

Each step of the lifecycle is briefly described here:

- **Performance Objectives**: Define performance SLOs/SLAs for the different scenarios.

- **Performance Modelling**: Identify business-critical workflows and transactions, and conduct modeling to understand performance-related implications.

- **Design Guidelines**: Prepare performance design guidelines, and suggest business workflow modifications if any.

- **Implement Design Guidelines**: Implement performance design guidelines within the solution components including instrumentation to capture metrics and conduct performance design reviews.

- **Performance Testing**: Conduct load/stress testing as per the load profile distribution to capture the metrics related to the health of the platform.

- **Bottleneck Analysis**: Identify, analyze, and remove bottlenecks in various components through code inspection and reviews.

- **Continuous Monitoring**: Establish continuous monitoring and alerting infrastructure as part of the DevOps processes.

- **Performance Governance**: Establish performance governance consisting of well-defined processes and teams to sustain the performance SLOs.

From the preceding section, we can understand that by adhering to a structured and disciplined approach, we can achieve the performance objectives for the API.

Let's look at a checklist of activities for development teams that can be used while preparing any task plans.

Checklist for development teams

Performance modeling, being an important activity, must be done meticulously to achieve the right outcomes. The focus on the goals and objectives at each stage of the development lifecycle is important. The following are important steps that development teams must follow:

1. Create a model for predicting performance. Capture both scalability requirements and the aspirational SLO definitions.

2. Add a user story for each performance-critical scenario under the features.

3. Create a performance model for each scenario – this performance model is input to the development team to ensure that the processing times for each step in the scenario are within the times allowed in the model.

4. Link the functional feature/user story with the performance user story for tracking.

5. Link performance test cases related to the critical scenario to the user story.

6. Use the status of the user story to track it as it moves from one state to another:

    a. **New**: Not yet approved by customer stakeholder

    b. **Approved**: Discussed and agreed by customer stakeholder

    c. **Verified**: Performance SLO verified using a performance test.

7. Design the system keeping performance objectives as an important criterion.

8. Implement and conduct performance tests on the solution to evaluate the application performance based on expected load conditions.

9. Analyze the findings to identify improvement areas.

10. Optimize performance and continuously monitor for issues.

The steps listed here are just a starting point, and you can expand on these to define a more detailed process for your teams.

Performance modeling is a very important activity that must be conducted seriously to derive the right architectural decisions. Seasonal increases in loads and other one-time business events may have a direct impact on the overall load on the platform.

Hence, all possible scalability requirements must be considered during the modeling activity to understand the constraints of the system. While the cloud is about elastic scale, there are upper limits to everything. API platforms can be implemented using a wide variety of Azure services. However, a thorough analysis of the pros and cons of each architecture approach is important to achieve the right level of scale and performance.

In the next section, we will look at patterns for ensuring the high availability of your API service.

High-availability patterns

High Availability (**HA**) is the ability of an application to continue running in a healthy state without significant downtime, absorbing temporary failures in dependent services and hardware. Most application strategies for high availability involve either redundancy or the removal of hard dependencies between application components. It is defined using the nines approach (for example, two nines = 99%, three nines = 99.9%, four nines = 99.99%, and so on).

For API platforms, the following strategies are typically adopted to offer high availability:

- **Load balancing across instances**: APIs will be designed to scale out by adding more instances. Load balancing strategies will improve resiliency by removing unhealthy instances out of rotation or service.

- **Geo-redundancy**: API platforms will be designed in a way that the Azure resources will be deployed in two geographically distributed locations so that an outage in one of the regions will not impact the availability of the API.

- **Using autoscaling to respond to increases in load**: The underlying Azure resources allocated for an API will be configured to scale out automatically as the load increases gradually.

- **Fault detection and retry logic**: The components within an API must detect transient failures and implement some sort of retry mechanism to make an attempt to complete the transaction.

- **Asynchronous communication and durable queues**: Asynchronous communication patterns reduce bottlenecks in distributed applications, thereby leading to the improved availability of the system.

  The messages (part of the request) are written to durable storage such as Azure Storage or Service Bus. In the event of transient failures within the processing pipeline, the messages are not lost. These will be retried after the service is back online.

Refer to the Azure Architecture center resources on building solutions for high availability: `https://docs.microsoft.com/en-us/azure/architecture/high-availability/building-solutions-for-high-availability`.

High-availability calculation

End-to-end HA for a cloud-based API solution is heavily dependent on the availability of the underlying building blocks or resources used for it. It is calculated as a multiplier of the availability numbers of each resource that is part of the request path.

For example, say an API platform is composed of four blocks, namely, the firewall, the gateway, the compute service for the hosting of the API, and the database.

The overall availability of the platform will be calculated as follows:

Availability = (availability of **Firewall**) x (availability of **Gateway**) x (availability of **Compute**) x (availability of **Database**)

So, let's say the individual availability numbers of the components were the following:

- Firewall: 99.9%
- Gateway: 99%
- Compute: 99.3%
- Database: 99.5%

Then the availability of the platform would be the following:

0.999 x 0.99 x 0.993 x 0.995 = 0.9771 = 97.71%

The calculations will change if there are multiple load-balanced paths. Thus, when designing API platforms, the architecture must consider the fact that the more components there are in the flow, the lower the availability of the platform will be.

In the next section, we will look at how to architect your API solution to include capabilities that would be beneficial for the operations and support team.

Architecting for operations

API platforms on the cloud are analogous to a distributed computing environment, making them relatively complex with a lot of moving parts. Further, transient failures of cloud resources are quite common and hence applications must be designed for resiliency. Hence, there is an imperative need to architect and design all modern applications with a *production-first* mindset.

Basically, the objective should be to bake in as much telemetry as possible, so that the operations team can monitor the site for any error conditions and then remediate any live site issues with proper root cause analysis. Two of the most important practices in this regard are the following:

- Logging, monitoring, and alerts
- Feature flags

Let's understand these in the next sections.

Logging, monitoring, and alerts

Logging and **monitoring** play a crucial role in the timely detection of issues and subsequent remedial action by the operations team. All API platforms must be designed with adequate logging and telemetry. In fact, it is a good development practice to incorporate as much logging as possible using various categories of log severity types, such as **Verbose, Information, Warning, Error,** and **Critical.** This way, developers can easily diagnose issues by tracing a request through the various loops and paths.

Application Performance Monitoring (**APM**) makes use of analytics from the captured logs to provide feedback to the development teams on the overall health of the application, including performance and usage.

Azure provides the ability to configure **alerts** based on specified preconditions as well. Operations support teams can respond to these alerts to restore the service back to normal conditions.

Learn more about best practices for monitoring in Azure here: `https://docs.microsoft.com/en-us/azure/architecture/best-practices/monitoring`.

Feature flags

Use feature flags for turning individual features on and off, which allows many small incremental versions of software to be delivered without the cost of constant branching and merging.

You can read more about feature flags here: `https://docs.microsoft.com/en-us/dotnet/architecture/cloud-native/feature-flags`.

Understanding maintainability

All software systems evolve over time. New enhancements and bug fixes must be planned and rolled out on a periodic basis. The term **maintainability** refers to the ease with which the software solution or component, or even a code file, can be modified or updated without incurring significant maintenance costs.

There are two major categorizations of maintainability: proactive and reactive.

Proactive maintainability

Proactive maintainability refers to the adherence to software development best practices while writing code for the various components of a solution. This includes both the **modularity** and **testability** of the components. The code should be easily changed without breaking the build or introducing any regression issues. In the longer term, it should be able to support enhancements with the addition of more features and capabilities.

Managing **technical debt** for a product is very important. Owing to numerous constraints, coding issues or design issues accumulate. These may manifest as bugs and disrupt the operation of a service. Hence, while technical debt is fixed as part of the code cleanup or refactoring activity, the business logic must not change. This will ensure that the service continues to function even after the changes have been incorporated.

Reactive maintainability

Reactive maintainability refers to the ability to repair and restore a service back to its normal operations after an incident has been registered. This is heavily dependent on the incident management procedures in place to respond to live site incidents. Postmortem analysis and other incident data analysis must be carried out to understand the root causes of issues. This is required to improve the system to eliminate the recurrence of similar incidents in the future.

Maintainability is linked to availability in the way that downtime is incurred due to maintainability, lowering the availability of the system.

In the next section, we will cover an approach for how to track your quality objectives and requirements using a quality dashboard.

Tracking objectives using a quality dashboard

It is recommended that API development teams should create a dashboard to track the quality attributes related to important business goals for a solution. These dashboards, also known as **quality dashboards**, provide a point-in-time view of the state of the solution with respect to the envisaged quality objectives. The data should be periodically reviewed and action items captured must be resolved to progressively improve the overall health of the solution.

A few of the important metrics that must be tracked using these dashboards are the following:

- An architecture backlog populated with quality-specific requirements and their respective lifecycle statuses

- The classification of bugs into non-functional categories and their statuses

- A count of automated tests and their test execution statuses

- The performance metrics of the solution

- Any other metrics as per the requirements of the key stakeholders

The objective of quality dashboards is to provide a snapshot of the top concerns that must be addressed by the project team to offer a highly reliable service.

So far in this chapter, you have gained an understanding of the important quality-related considerations that apply to API architectures. In the next section, we will expand on our case study and apply the concepts presented in this chapter to assure the quality of the API product.

Case study elaboration – Packt Insurance Inc.

Let's now work through the case study and see what steps are to be taken by the team at Packt Insurance to achieve quality expectations for the solution. Through discussions with the various stakeholders and business teams at Packt Insurance, the development team captured the following high-level requirements:

- The solution should be multi-tenant and deployed initially in one Azure region. It should be easy to replicate the deployment in other Azure regions.

- Deployments to production environments will be fully automated and the cycle time will be 2-3 weeks max.

- Automated tests must be run on the APIs to check for regression issues before they are released to production.

- The public endpoints for the APIs must be secured through OAuth.

- The API platform will not store any encrypted data. The highest classification of data handled by the platform will be **Confidential / High Business Impact**. The platform will handle PII data and must comply with country-specific laws.

- All APIs must respond within 3-5 seconds; read calls must be faster than updates.

- All APIs must support at least 20 RPS (average) and peak traffic of 50 RPS (maximum).

- A monitoring and alert mechanism should be in place to notify the support team whenever health degradation happens.

- In the event of a disaster, the recovery time objective will be 8 hours, and the recovery point objective will be 1 hour.

> **Note:**
> A few of the quality requirements will be addressed through DevOps practices. Those are discussed in *Chapter 7, Accelerating through DevOps Essentials.*

Important SLOs for the API platform

For the Packt Insurance Inc. API platform, the development team came up with the following SLOs:

- 95% of all READ requests will be responded to within 1 second aggregated over a 1-day period.

- 95% of all CREATE/UPDATE requests will be responded to within 3 seconds.

- 99% of all requests will be responded to within 5 seconds without any failures.

- 99.9% of all requests will succeed within a 5-minute window.

- 99% of requests during the peak 1-hour window will be successful.

- Less than 1% of requests will error out during the peak 1-hour period.

The Packt Insurance development team will adjust the design of the API platform to achieve these goals.

Architecture backlog – focus on quality and handle technical debt

Architecture backlog refers to the set of stories that do not address the needs of an end user persona directly. However, they are created to address technical risks and issues, as well as to clean up any technical debt. Hence, while measuring the velocity of the teams, a certain amount of capacity should be set aside to handle the architecture backlog stories.

Packt Insurance Inc. created an architectural backlog. The team used Azure DevOps as its work tracking system. They created **Epic** as the architecture and added features and stories underneath it:

		Order	Work Item Type	ID	Title		State
⊞ ⊟							
+		1	Epic	1168	⌄ 👑 Architecture	⋯	● New
			Feature	1173	› 🏆 Design		● New
			Feature	1182	› 🏆 Information Security		● New
			Feature	1184	› 🏆 Infrastructure		● New
			Feature	1195	› 🏆 Testing		● New
			Feature	1238	› 🏆 Telemetry & Operational Insights		● New
			Feature	2598	› 🏆 Security - Threat Modelling		● New
			Feature	2599	› 🏆 Security - AuthN/AuthZ		● New
			Feature	2600	› 🏆 Scalability - Compute		● New
			Feature	2601	› 🏆 Scalability - Data		● New
			Feature	2602	› 🏆 Performance - Modelling		● New
			Feature	2603	› 🏆 Performance - Measurement		● New
			Feature	2604	› 🏆 Performance - Automated Testing		● New
			Feature	2605	› 🏆 High Availability		● New
			Feature	2606	› 🏆 BCP & Disaster Recovery		● New

Figure 4.6 – Sample representative architecture backlog view in DevOps

The Packt Insurance development team identified an initial list of prioritized architectural stories during Sprint 0. During the initial sprints, the team will expand the features and add more stories to meet the various SLOs and other quality-related metrics for the platform.

> **Note**
>
> The backlog depicted in the preceding section is not meant to be an exhaustive list. The central idea here is to emphasize on the point that all project teams must create a backlog of architecture stories to track various non-functional requirements and take them through the lifecycle stages of design, development, and testing for closure.

What we have presented as part of this case study is only a minimum starting point. You are encouraged to apply your real project experiences, further ideate on these, and identify additional improvements or considerations that may be necessary to build a great API product.

Summary

In this chapter, you reviewed, purely from an architecture standpoint, how quality requirements are critical to the success of the API platform. Hence, it is pertinent to recommend that, during the API development lifecycle stages, you prioritize any architectural stories that are part of the backlog, along with any functional stories. This, however, requires executive buy-in for the strategy, and manpower investment to support the approach. Quality outcomes are dependent on the culture of the team.

We also briefly touched on the topics of API security, reliability, availability, and performance. You now understand how maintainability is linked to availability and reliability, and why you must be careful about your choice of the appropriate levels of reliability.

There is always a trade-off between cost optimization, performance, and reliability. Hence, you should evangelize within your teams on how optimal service reliability can be achieved by adopting SRE practices. Building software with a production mindset is a total paradigm shift for development teams. It requires a good amount of discipline and honest and intentional effort to be successful at that.

In the next chapter, we will go over RESTful APIs – the new web standard.

Further reading

- ISO/IEC 25010:2011 specification: `https://www.iso.org/standard/35733.html`
- ISO 25010 definitions: `https://iso25000.com/index.php/en/iso-25000-standards/iso-25010?start=0`
- Azure Well-Architected Framework: `https://docs.microsoft.com/en-us/azure/architecture/framework/`
- Architecture Tradeoff Analysis: `https://www.geeksforgeeks.org/architecture-tradeoff-analysis-method-atam/`
- Architecture Assessment: `https://itabok.iasaglobal.org/architecture-assessment/?mc_cid=26b6a7c986&mc_eid=1ce5922cf6`

- Microsoft Security Development Lifecycle: `https://www.microsoft.com/en-us/securityengineering/sdl/`

- Site Reliability Engineering: `https://docs.microsoft.com/en-us/azure/site-reliability-engineering/`

- Engineering for Performance: `https://docs.microsoft.com/en-us/previous-versions/msp-n-p/ff647781(v=pandp.10)`

- Significant benefits of SRE: `https://blog.goodelearning.com/subject-areas/devops/what-are-the-most-significant-benefits-of-search-reliability-engineering-sre/`

5
RESTful APIs – the New Web

For most enterprises, using industry-accepted implementation standards is critical for ensuring a consistent experience across the catalog of APIs that are deployed. Adhering to one common standard simplifies the development and deployment processes, thereby ensuring **reliability** and **maintainability**. While there may be an initial learning curve for the team, but these investments will yield better results with the broad spectrum of experience within the development teams.

The purpose of this chapter is to look at the **REST** standard, which builds upon the **Hypertext Transfer Protocol** (**HTTP**) standard. The REST API style is the most popular standard and is commonly used in all modern applications. REST is becoming a new web standard and is being adopted as an **OpenAPI Standard** by most organizations, including cloud platform service providers. The cloud services natively support REST API endpoints that can be used for various operations, including administrating the respective platform services in a consistent manner.

We will also briefly touch on the benefits of using RESTful APIs, as well as how to leverage the existing tools to quickly design and produce documentation for discovery, and publishing the API.

As such, we are going to cover the following main topics:

- Understanding RESTful APIs
- REST architecture constraints
- Advantages and challenges of building a RESTful API
- Exploring the checklist for building RESTful APIs
- OpenAPI Specification

By the end of this chapter, you will understand the important technical design considerations to be kept in mind while building RESTful APIs for the enterprise.

> **Note**
>
> This chapter is not meant to serve as a comprehensive guide on the REST API standard. Please make use of the references at the end of this chapter to augment your understanding of the topic.

Technical requirements

There are no specific technical requirements for this chapter. However, to understand a few concepts presented here, it will be useful to have access to the following:

- Visual Studio Code (`https://code.visualstudio.com/`)
- Postman (`https://www.postman.com/`)

The code from this chapter can be found on GitHub at `https://github.com/PacktPublishing/Designing-API-First-Enterprise-Architectures-on-Azure/tree/main/Chapter5`

Understanding RESTful APIs

The term **REST** is an acronym for **REpresentational State Transfer**, which is an architectural style for creating web services that comply with a set of rules and constraints. REST only uses a subset of the HTTP protocol standard, so is quite popular among the developer community for building backend services that offer flexibility in the way data (resources) can be accessed.

As we discussed in *Chapter 3, Architecture Principles and API Styles*, a REST-based architecture system can be visualized as having two parts; namely, the **client**, who requests the resources, and the **server**, which has the resources:

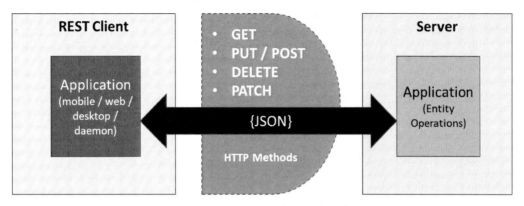

Figure 5.1 – REST architecture style

> **Note**
>
> When using REST APIs, different data formats are supported, such as XML, YAML, or any other machine-readable format. However, JSON is the most preferred and commonly used format.

HTTP-based web services that adhere to the REST guidelines are known as **RESTful APIs**. These APIs use existing HTTP methodologies defined by the RFC 2616 protocol to process client requests. You can find more details on RFC 2616 here: `https://www.w3.org/Protocols/rfc2616/rfc2616.html`.

When using the REST standard, please keep the following in mind:

- All interactions between the client and server are message-based, and the HTTP standard is used to describe these messages.

- All interactions follow a simple request/response mechanism. A request will always receive a response, even if there was an error. HTTP status codes are used to denote the outcome of the request.

There are five methods that are commonly used in an HTTP REST-based architecture; they are, **POST**, **GET**, **PUT**, **PATCH**, and **DELETE**. These correspond to the **create**, **read, update**, and **delete** (or **CRUD**) operations of the representative business object, respectively. The business object allows us to abstract over the underlying system. There are other methods that are less frequently used, such as **OPTIONS** and **HEAD**.

The following data formats are supported by REST APIs:

- `application/json`
- `application/xml`
- `application/x-wbe+xml`
- `application/x-www-form-urlencoded`
- `multipart/form-data`

In the next section, you will learn how to correctly use HTTP verbs while defining your API operations, along with the expected status codes. It is important for developers to understand the usage of the API, and interpret the response that's received.

Using HTTP verbs for your CRUD actions correctly

REST API operations are always modeled as one of the HTTP operations. A mapping between the HTTP verbs and the respective CRUD action is depicted here. Keep this in mind while preparing the interface definition of your API. The behaviors and actions of the entity must be correctly mapped by using HTTP verbs:

HTTP Verb	CRUD Action	Purpose	Expected Status Codes
POST	Create	Create a new record in the underlying system using the data available in the request body.	201 (Created), "Location" header with a link to /customers/{id} containing new ID. 404 (Not Found). 409 (Conflict) if the resource already exists.
GET	Read	Retrieves one or more records based on the request URI. The information may also be optionally served from the cache. MUST NOT modify any data.	200 (OK), list of customers / single customer. Use pagination, sorting, and filtering to navigate big lists. 404 (Not Found), if ID not found or invalid.
PUT	Update/ Replace	Update or replace an existing resource.	200 (OK) or 204 (No Content). 404 (Not Found), if the ID is not found or invalid. 405 (Method Not Allowed), unless you want to update/replace every resource in the entire collection.
PATCH	Update/ Modify	Update or modify an existing resource in the underlying system.	200 (OK) or 204 (No Content). 404 (Not Found), if the ID is not found or invalid. 405 (Method Not Allowed), unless you want to modify the collection itself.
DELETE	Delete	Delete an existing record on the server, as specified by the request URI. A proper HTTP response must be returned to the caller to indicate whether the delete operation succeeded.	200 (OK). 404 (Not Found), if the ID is not found or invalid. 405 (Method Not Allowed), unless you want to delete the whole collection – not often desirable.

Knowledge check – How well do you know the HTTP standard?

Designing APIs the REST way requires having a good understanding of the HTTP standard and its associated concepts. Please make use of the references provided in *the Further reading* section.

In the next section, we will briefly touch on the history and evolution of inter-machine application communication techniques.

History of inter-machine application communication

With the growth of the internet, there was a pressing need to open the boundaries of communication among the components/parts of a distributed system. Around early 2000, client-server-type applications started communicating over HTTP, which lead to the adoption of new standards such as **Simple Object Access Protocol (SOAP)** and **Web Services Description Language (WSDL)**. Legacy n-tier applications that had been built using CORBA/COM+/DCOM/RPC had to be redesigned to allow the business tier to be exposed as HTTP web services.

As more API-based services/applications started emerging, REST-style architectures became more popular. Software developers found the standard quite easy to use and adopt (even when compared to SOAP web services):

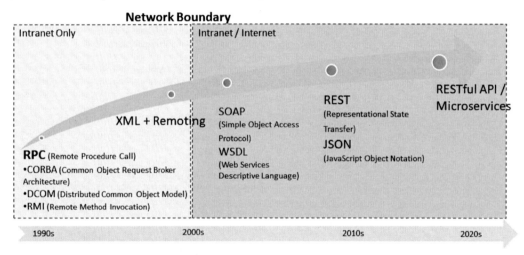

Figure 5.2 – History of inter-machine communication techniques

Despite the popularity of REST, newer protocols such as **Graph Query Language (GraphQL)** and **Open Source Remote Procedure Call**, originally developed by Google (**gRPC**), are also gaining in popularity, however, the REST-based API style has remained the most preferred technique while building data-driven API services. In fact, many of the new architecture styles that make use of the HTTP protocol are only an extension of the REST standard.

In the next section, we will review some of the constraints that are imposed by the REST architecture style.

REST architecture constraints

In *Chapter 3, Architecture Principles and API Styles*, we discussed different architecture styles and their use, depending on the use case's suitability. The REST architecture style, though widely adopted, has a few limitations that must be understood properly before you decide to use this style. These limitations merely stem from the guidance around building strictly RESTful APIs. But within an enterprise, it is quite likely that deviations may exist due to standards not being interpreted properly by the development teams. It's important to understand what makes a REST API truly *RESTful*, and why these constraints exist, before building your API.

In general, there are primarily six key constraints that apply while building RESTful APIs:

- **Uniform interface**: This is the key constraint that differentiates a REST API from other types of API implementations. It revolves around the idea that HTTPzzbased services can be seen as web resources, and there may be a uniform way of interacting with and accessing those resources, irrespective of the type of client application (desktop or mobile). This strategy of decoupling a client (typically, a UI application) from its backend API service (hosted in a separate server) allows the application to evolve independently, without having the application's services, models, and actions, being tightly coupled to the API layer itself. All the clients consume the published uniform interface for communication.

  There are four guidelines that are part of the *Uniform Interface* principle. They are as follows:

  a) **Resource-based**: It should be possible to distinguish and identify the resource based on the request. The naming convention that's followed for the URL paths must clearly state the resource being requested.

  An example is APIs/customers.

  b) **Manipulating resources through representations**: The client has received a representation of a resource and has information about the various operations, such as delete or update, that may be performed on the resource based on access permissions.

  An example of this is DELETE API/Customer/<Customer Id>.

c) **Self-descriptive messages**: The messages that are received by the server are self-contained and informative enough to describe the message so that it can be processed easily by the server.

d) **Hypermedia as the Engine of Application State (HATEOAS)**: The response can contain additional links to direct the client to other resource URIs for requesting additional information about the specific resource.

- **Client-server model**: In a distributed application environment, the client-server model refers to separating tasks between two systems or applications; namely, the server and the client. The client sends a request to the server to fetch data or execute an action, while the server receives the request and further executes the function as requested.

  The REST style architecture is analogous to the **client-server** architecture. This constraint operates on the concept that the client and the server should be separate from each other and allowed to evolve individually. The server application provides a layer of abstraction over the underlying logic and data layer. The client applications that initiate the operations on the server do not know about the logic, nor does the server application know anything about the client frontend app.

- **Stateless**: REST APIs are stateless. This means that calls can be made independently of one another. The client must include all the information and data that's necessary to complete the request on the server. The clients can pass this as part of the query parameters, headers, and URI. This feature of statelessness offers high availability for the API service as it no longer needs to maintain or manage the state of the client. However, as a drawback, it requires the client to send too much information to the server. This reduces any scope for network optimization and usually requires more bandwidth.

- **Cacheable**: The output response of a REST API request can be cached on the client. Each response should include information (typically, in response headers) to indicate whether the response is cacheable and the overall duration for which the response can be cached on the client. Due to its stateless nature, a REST API may require scalability to handle large loads of incoming and outbound calls. Hence, it is recommended that caching best practices are followed while designing and implementing the API, to avoid unnecessary round trips.

- **Layered system**: REST APIs usually have different layers as part of their architecture. These individual layers have specific purposes and work cohesively to build a hierarchy that helps create a more scalable and modular application. The modularity and extensibility of the API depends on the number of layers. Data exchange across layers happens through a published data model or data contract.

- **Code on demand**: Code on demand is an optional feature of REST and allows code to be transmitted via the API for use within the application. Examples of code on demand may include compiled components such as Java applets and client-side scripts such as JavaScript. However, this is a rarely used feature of REST. Hence, this constraint does not apply to most of the REST API implementations.

In the next section, you will explore the benefits and challenges of using the RESTful API style within your API-centric solutions.

Advantages and challenges of building a RESTful API

There are a few advantages, as well as common challenges, when it comes to building RESTful APIs. These advantages and challenges will be explained in detail in the following subsections.

Advantages

The RESTful API style offers significant advantages compared to other styles. Hence, when it comes to building API-based enterprise applications, the REST standard is the most preferred specification in the IT industry.

The main benefits are as follows:

- **Scalability**: This is the most important quality when you're adopting the REST standard. Owing to the separation between the client and the server, the development teams can plan to scale up/out the REST APIs, independent of how the clients will consume it. This concept of separation of concerns, coupled with stateless design, facilitates the development of APIs that are modular in nature. Each of the APIs can be scaled independently, as per requirements.

- **Flexibility and portability**: Since the API layer is designed to provide abstraction over the backend database, this serves as a repository pattern, allowing database changes to be incorporated without impacting the clients. It makes adopting the REST standard flexible and portable.

- **Independence**: The REST standard is an independent platform and can be implemented by different technology platforms and programming languages. Different project teams, as per the available skillset within their respective teams, can independently develop RESTful APIs. This can then be easily integrated as part of the larger ecosystem of APIs within the enterprise.

- **Easy to learn**, **understand**, and **implement**: The REST API standard is quite easy to follow and use since it is based on the HTTP standard, which is typically used to build web services. The rules for building a REST API are mostly limited to CRUD-based operations, so it can be easily implemented using any programming language.

- **Supports both JSON** and **XML**: REST APIs can support both JSON and XML as data formats for exchanging information. Hence, this makes it quite powerful to integrate both a legacy API (using XML) and modern APIs (using JSON). API developers can accomplish capabilities that SOAP-based web services can.

- **Discoverability**: Owing to the fact that the REST style uses mostly CRUD operations, the API definition is easy to read and understand by API consumers. The client apps can easily integrate with it, whether it was originally designed for it or not.

- **Authorization**: REST APIs bring in standard-based verification using the `OAuth` protocol as it requires authorization tokens to be sent in the request header.

Next, let's look at some of the common challenges faced while using RESTful APIs.

Common challenges

It is a well-known fact that the benefits outweigh the risks associated with using the REST API style for your enterprise applications. Often, application developers lack complete knowledge, leading to perceptions that may impair their ability to develop proper RESTful APIs.

Hence, it is imperative that the challenges are understood properly, to avoid any confusion about the topic. Some of them are listed as follows:

- **URI paths and endpoint consistency**: All the paths and URIs for the endpoints must be consistent, as per the standard, but this may be difficult to manage when new capabilities must be introduced.

- **API versioning**: Having a proper versioning strategy is important while building REST APIs. Otherwise, any existing integrations may cause breaking as there may be functional and structural updates for an API whenever a new version is released.

- **Payload size**: As the standard suggests, a full entity object must be returned. The overall payload can be high for complex entity types, leading to low throughput due to an increased response time on the server.

- **Limited support for user input**: REST uses URL paths for input parameters, so it is limited by the navigation and paths supported by the URIs.

- **Error handling**: Owing to the fact that we can use HTTP status codes as part of our response codes, the error handling mechanism must be robust. There must be a way to differentiate successful or valid operations with error states. Client applications must be able to differentiate between the error status codes. Otherwise, the user experience will be drastically impacted as users will not know what happened with the request.

- **API testing**: The API testing strategy is sometimes complex because a certain sequence must be followed while testing the APIs. Since the APIs are operations over an underlying business system, there must be provisioning for synthetic transactions so that the database is not loaded with unnecessary records, since the tests may be run continuously. You can make use of design patterns such as Template or Proxy for this. API testing is critical for detecting build breaks due to enhancements, or new features being rolled out.

- **Authentication**: APIs only support the methods (Basic, OAuth, JSON Web Tokens, and so on) that are allowed as part of the `Authorize` header of the HTTP request.

The points listed here must be thoroughly discussed within the team very early in the life cycle. This is critical for developing a common understanding within the team and establishing the list of standards that will be followed.

In the next section, we will review the recommended practices for building a RESTful API.

Exploring the checklist for building RESTful APIs

Cloud computing and microservices are almost certain to follow RESTful API design as a rule for its implementations. The stateless nature of these APIs allows these services to be redeployed easily, whenever they're needed.

The following tables serve as a design and implementation checklist for all RESTful API developers:

- **Model domain actions using HTTP methods**: Earlier in this chapter, you understood that the operations that are supported by a REST API can be modeled as HTTP operations on a specified resource. Hence, it is a common practice to enumerate the various actions that will be allowed on a domain entity, and then map those different HTTP methods to indicate the operation to be performed on the requested resource, as identified by the request URI:

HTTP Method	Description
DELETE	HTTP request method used to remove the item.
GET	HTTP request method used to retrieve the last saved representation of a resource's state.
HEAD	HTTP request method used to retrieve the metadata associated with the resource.
OPTIONS	HTTP request method used to retrieve the metadata that describes the resource's available interactions.
POST	HTTP request method used to create a new resource within a collection or execute a controller.
PUT	HTTP request method that can also be used to insert a new resource into a store. This can also be used to update/replace a mutable resource in the store.
PATCH	HTTP request method used to update or modify an existing resource.

- **Ensure that all the supported features are CRUD in nature**: RESTful APIs typically update any backend database system. Hence, all the supported operations must be linked to one of the CRUD operations on the database system. When dealing with complex hierarchical objects or domain entities, the API operation can execute CRUD on one or more underlying database objects.

- **Use the proper HTTP status codes**: REST APIs are typically request-response pairs. Hence, HTTP status codes must be used to denote the outcome of the action, even if it was a failure.

The most commonly used HTTP codes are as follows:

Code	Name	Meaning
200	OK	Sent when the request was successfully processed.
201	Received	Sent when the request was received at the server. Typically used for asynchronous API implementations.
400	Bad Request	Indicates a non-specific client error.
401	Unauthorized	Sent when the client provided invalid credentials or a token or forgot to send them.
402	Forbidden	Sent to deny access to a specific resource.
404	Not Found	Sent when the client tried to interact with a URI that the REST API could not map to a resource.
405	Method Not Allowed	Sent when the client tried to interact using an unsupported HTTP method.
406	Not Acceptable	Sent when the client tried to request data in an unsupported media type format.
409	Conflict	Indicates that the client tried to violate the request state.
412	Precondition Failed	Tells the client that one of the preconditions was not met.
415	Unsupported Media Type	Sent when the client submitted data in a supported format or media type.
500	Internal Server Error	Tells the client that the API is having problems of its own.

The following are a few best practices that your development teams must follow:

- **Use a document serialized object for HTTP bodies**: Typically, the request body or response output of an API (in JSON or XML format) must conform to the serialized representation of the business entity objects. This eliminates the need for additional processing, such as unwrapping or formats being converted by the client on the response that's received.

- **Make use of HTTP headers to serve additional metadata**: It is important to make use of HTTP headers appropriately to contain additional metadata about the resource under consideration for the API. This metadata information can be used for a variety of purposes and can serve as important attributes for intermediary components such as firewalls.

Some commonly used headers are as follows:

a) **Content-Type**: This identifies the media type for the entire body.

b) **Content-Length**: This is the entire body's size in bytes.

c) **Last-Modified**: This shows the date and time of the last event changed on the requested resource.

d) **Etag**: Indicates the response message entity's version. You can read more about this here: `https://www.geeksforgeeks.org/what-is-http-etag/`.

e) **Cache-Control**: This is a caching value that is **Time to Live (TTL)**-based (in seconds).

f) **Location**: This provides the requested resource's URI.

- **API documentation**: One of the best practices is to document your REST API with as many details as possible while covering HTTP methods, URIs, HTTP status codes, and request/response entity schema definitions. This makes the API easy to use for developers while they're building the client applications. With the emergence of industry standards such as the OpenAPI Specification or JSON API, there are a lot of tools that can be used to create API definitions and documentation. You can make use of the references provided in the *Further reading* section to read more about this.

- **Authorization policy**: Since security is the most important thing for any API implementation, developers must implement the appropriate checks for authorization within their API implementation. This can involve both role-based and attributed-based access policies that must be satisfied before the API allows the caller to execute the necessary actions. For example, say the profile of a user can only be updated by the user. Hence, the API must implement a check to ensure that only the current user can update their respective profile information.

- **Faster and optimized response time**: REST APIs that are mostly used for synchronous operations usually have higher response times compared to asynchronous ones. This is primarily because heavy-duty processing is happening as part of the same operation context, so the various dependencies, such as other external API calls, and data conversions and save, can impact the overall wait period before a response is sent back to the client. Hence, the right analysis must be done to reduce all bottlenecks. It is recommended to target faster response times (less than a second) from the very beginning as well. Ensure that the appropriate telemetry is in place to capture the response time metric and raise alarms whenever significant deviations are observed.

- **Use a URI to handle hierarchical or nested relationships**: As the underlying business domain could be complex, there is a possibility that the core entity may be associated with multiple other entities, either as a parent-child relationship or as linked objects. Hence, the URI patterns must be designed while keeping this under consideration and return the data for the appropriate relationship level. Sometimes, the URI paths can be a little complex when iterating through multiple nested relationships.

  For example, say the `/api/policies/id` URI returned the policy resource for the specified ID. Then, the `/api/policies/id/assets` URI will return all the assets that were linked to the respective policy. Thus, URI subpaths can serve as individual operations on the requested resource.

- **Consistent naming and formatting guidelines**: To keep all your API interfaces clean and consistent, proper naming and casing techniques must be followed while naming the various entities and operations. The standard convention is to make use of plural names for the object in the URI to serve as the root of the collection.

  For example, `/api/quotes/`, `/api/policies/`, and `/api/claims/` indicate the respective collection objects. Having a `GET` on `/api/policies/id` will get the policy document for the specified `id` value.

- **Sorting, filtering, and pagination**: For most enterprise applications, the REST API endpoints will be dealing with large datasets on the backend. Hence, operations such as **sorting**, **filtering**, and **pagination** are important to narrow down the results to a limited set that is of relevance to the clients. Otherwise, the resultant datasets for listing operations could be quite huge and complex, thereby impacting the overall performance of the API operation.

  Different query string parameters are used for the purpose of sorting, filtering, and paging. For example, `?sort="name asc"` indicates that we can apply sorting on the `name` attribute in descending fashion. Likewise, the `?publisher="*Packt*"` parameter will do a wildcard search and try to find all the records that contain the word `packt` in the publisher attribute. Similarly, parameters such as `?offset=0&limit=10` will retrieve the top 10 records at **start at index** 0 for the specified criteria.

  You must consider all these requirements as part of the API design to consistently follow and implement them.

- **Prefer JSON for the payload**: JSON format is widely accepted as an industry standard for REST APIs. It allows a flexible schema to be used that can be modified with full backward compatibility support. Adhering to other standards, such as SOAP XML, can make your interfaces tightly coupled, which may make them difficult to integrate with. Hence, within an enterprise context, most of the APIs tend to make use of JSON as the default standard.

- **Must include automated API testing**: It is a common practice to write API tests to verify REST interfaces. These tests are easier to write and simulate using a wide variety of tools. They can also serve as documentation that indicates how the API endpoints can be invoked from a variety of languages and platforms.

  The tests are also useful for validating whether the API works as expected post any changes or upgrades.

Now that you have reviewed the important practices that all development teams must follow while building their REST APIs, let's review the importance of defining your REST API contracts before the implementation has started.

Contract-first design for your REST APIs

Contract-first design refers to the technique of identifying the contract definitions for your REST API. This includes both the interfaces and operations that are available, along with their respective data types and response structures.

This originated from the concept of using a WSDL file to define a web service. For REST APIs, this is documented using other techniques, such as the OpenAPI Specification. The objective is to describe the operations supported by the API so that they can be shared with the API consumers for implementing the integration points.

There are many benefits of using the contract-first approach:

- You can implement client integrations in parallel with the API development.

- The contract serves as a baseline for the list of operations that are supported. The development teams can write client-side unit tests to mock the operations.

- The contracts are agreements between the consumer (client app) and the provider (API) and are cross-platform-compatible. Development teams can make use of different languages to build the different components of the solution.

In the next section, we will explore the OpenAPI Specification, which is quite popular for constructing the API interface definition file. This file will act as the contract of the API.

OpenAPI Specification

The **OpenAPI Specification** (**OAS**) defines a standard that can be used to create the interface definition of a RESTful API in a language-agnostic manner. This allows the consumers of the API, whether they're humans or computers, to easily decipher the capabilities of the services without requiring access to source code, documentation, or even inspections of the network traffic. Owing to its wide acceptance in the community, APIs that are defined properly using the specification constructs will be readily available for use by the developers planning to integrate with the API.

There are a variety of developer productivity tools that can parse the OpenAPI definition files, as well as display the API specification in a graphical manner that is easy to understand and follow. There are tools that can generate stubs or proxy classes using these definition files or even in API testing, using mocks.

You can read more about the OpenAPI Specification at `https://spec.openapis.org/oas/v3.1.0`.

OpenAPI definition file format

OpenAPI definition files, also popularly known as swagger files, for a RESTful API can be constructed in either JSON or YAML format. The swagger file is used to define the entire API. This includes information about the endpoints, the operations that are supported, how parameters can be passed, error schemas, authorization methods, and more.

At the time of writing, v3.0 of the specification is in use. The structure of the file is depicted in the following diagram:

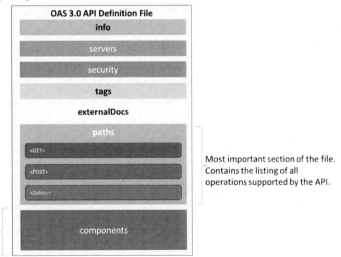

Figure 5.3 – OpenAPI v3.0 file structure

Let's explore how we can quickly create the API definition file for one of the APIs, namely the Policy API for the Packt Insurance Inc. solution that we discussed in the previous chapters.

You can construct the API definition file in just seven steps. They are as follows:

1. Capture the basic **information** about the API:

```
openapi: '3.0.2'
info:
   title: Policy API
   description: API endpoint for the Policy subsystem
   version: '1.0'
```

2. Specify the **server** URL hosting the API service:

```
servers:
   - url: https://api.packt.com/v1
```

3. Mention the **security** requirements that must be adhered to by consumers:

```
security:
   - api_auth:
     - write:policy
     - read:policy
```

4. Specify any **tags** that may be useful for the API discovery:

```
tags:
   - name: Policy API
```

5. Give reference to `externalDocs` for additional information about the API:

```
externalDocs:
   url: https://api-docs.packt.com/apis/policyapis
   description: developer documentation of the policy api
```

6. Define the operations and paths supported by the API:

```
paths:
  /policies:
    post:
      tags:
```

```
        - Create Policy
    summary: Create a Policy
    description: creates a policy based on the
        information passed.
    operation: createpolicy
    request Body:
      description: Policy Document Object
      content:
        application/json:
          schema:
            $ref:  "#/components/schemas/
PolicyDocument"
    responses:
      200:
        description: id of the policy record
        content:
          application/text:
            schema:
              type: string
  get:
    tags:
      - Get Policies
    summary: Get the collection of Policies.
    description: returns a list of policies in the
        system.
    operationId: getpolicy
    parameters:
      - name: limit
        in: query
        description: 'count of records to be returned'
        required: false
        schema:
          type: integer
          default: 100
      - name: offset
        in: query
```

```
              description: 'starting offset for the query.'
              required: false
              schema:
                type: integer
                default: 0
          responses:
            200:
              description: Collection of Policies
              content:
                application/json:
                  schema:
                    $ref:   "#/components/schemas/Policies"
  /policies/{id}:
    parameters:
      - name: id
        in: path
        description: 'Id of the policy record'
        required: true
        schema:
          type: integer
    get:
      tags:
        - Policy by Id
      summary: Get the Policy by Id
      description: returns the specified policy.
      operationId: getpolicybyid
      responses:
        200:
          description: Policy Document
          content:
            application/json:
              schema:
                $ref:
                    "#/components/schemas/PolicyDocument"
        402:
          description: Unauthorized access
```

```
            content:
              application/text:
                schema:
                  type: string
                  example: User is not allowed to access
                    this policy.
          404:
            description: Not found.
            content:
              application/text:
                schema:
                  type: string
                  example: The specified policy does not
                      exist.
```

7. Define the schema of the various data `components` used by the API:

```
  components:
    schemas:
      Policies:
        type: array
        items:
          properties:
            PolicyDocument:
              type: object
              properties:
                policyId:
                  type: string
                  example: "POL-COMP-1234567-I"
                dateissued:
                  type: string
      PolicyDocument:
        type: object
        properties:
            policyId:
              type: string
```

```
                        example: "POL-COMP-1234567-I"
                customerId:
                    type: string
                    example: "IND123459873457CR"
                dateissued:
                    type: string
    securitySchemes:
        name:
            type: oauth2
            flows:
                authorizationCode:
                    authorizationUrl:
                        'https://login.microsoftonline.com/<tenant-
                        id>/oauth2/v2.0/token'
                    tokenUrl:
                        'https://login.microsoftonline.com/<tenant-
                        id>/oauth2/v2.0/token'
                    scopes:
                        read:policy: read
                write:policy: write
```

8. With that, you've seen how easy it is to create API definition files.

In the next section, we will look at how easy it is to visualize a swagger definition file using **Visual Studio Code (VSCode)**.

Visualizing the API definition file using the Swagger extension in VSCode

Various tools are available for authoring OpenAPI Specification files. Here, we have made use of Visual Studio Code, along with OpenAPI Editing and Swagger viewer plugins, to construct and verify the structure of the file.

The following screenshot shows what this looks like overall:

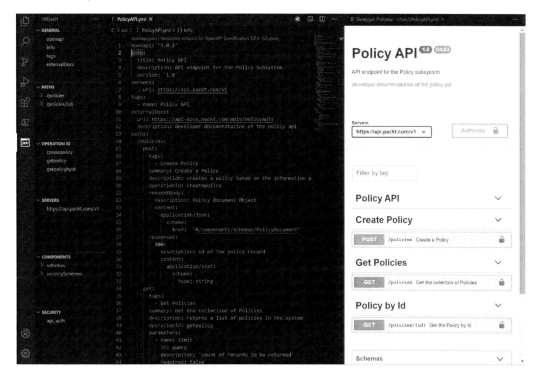

Figure 5.4 – Policy API Swagger definition file

A properly structured and well-documented RESTful API is a delight for all the consumers of the API. It is of the utmost importance for all public APIs. Hence, sufficient attention and time must be allocated to construct the interface definition in a professional manner.

Summary

In this chapter, you reviewed how RESTful APIs are quite easy to use and adapt. You also studied the constraints and limitations that must be kept in mind while designing APIs for your enterprise.

As REST APIs are becoming the new web standard, it is important that you delve deep into the concepts of REST by making use of the links provided in the *Further reading* section. It takes a few iterations and experiments to fully understand this style before you can put it to use.

By incorporating the best practices, you can create an API that is easily understood and consistent with the intended purpose. The developer community can take advantage of API offerings with a reduced learning curve since, overall, the RESTful style is the most convenient and easier one to integrate with.

Coupled with additional capabilities such as self-service API enablement through API Discovery Portals, enterprises can tap into the enormous potential and opportunities of the marketplace.

In the next chapter, we will look at some of the best practices for designing and implementing API-centric solutions.

Further reading

- Hypertext Transfer Protocol: `https://www.w3.org/Protocols/rfc2616/rfc2616.html`

- Microsoft API Building Guidelines: `https://github.com/Microsoft/api-guidelines/blob/vNext/Guidelines.md`

- Definition of the REST Standard: `https://en.wikipedia.org/wiki/Representational_state_transfer`

- REST API Design Rule Book: `https://www.oreilly.com/library/view/rest-api-design/9781449317904/`

- Tutorial on the REST API: `https://restfulapi.net/`

- REST API Design Guidelines: `https://searchapparchitecture.techtarget.com/tip/16-REST-API-design-best-practices-and-guidelines`

- Open API Detailed Specification: `https://www.openapis.org/`

- Open API Specification Examples: `https://github.com/OAI/OpenAPI-Specification`

- JSON API Specification: `https://jsonapi.org/`

6
API Design Practices

APIs are a company's greatest digital asset. Modern applications rely heavily on these backend services to realize their amazing digital experiences. Successful API platforms can capture customers, while the bad ones will be a liability, resulting in a lot of support calls. Hence, adhering to good design and implementation practices is critical to ensuring you have a quality product. Public APIs carry the inherent risk of impacting brand reputation if not done right.

A good API is one that is easy to understand, simple to use, easy to maintain and extend, and provides output as per the expectation of the audience. Careful planning and a well-thought-through design and implementation approach that considers all the requirements are strongly recommended before you write any code. Also, development practices such as test-driven development may be useful in detecting any issues at the early stages.

The purpose of this chapter is to focus on the important aspects that must be considered as part of designing and implementing API services.

In this chapter, we are going to cover the following main topics:

- Understanding API design considerations
- Exploring recommended practices
- Implementing an API service using design patterns
- Developer toolbox

> **Tip – Sequence diagrams**
>
> Sequence diagrams are very useful in depicting request-response flows. It aids in capturing all the subsystems that will be involved as part of the complete business operation. For most of your critical flows, performing analysis using sequence diagrams will aid in discovering dependencies, performance bottlenecks, and resource constraints. Furthermore, there are tools such as PlantUML (`https://plantuml.com/sequence-diagram`) that allow you to create and maintain sequence diagrams, similar to code, that can be checked into your GitHub repository alongside the API module code.

Understanding API design considerations

The API design process involves analyzing the business and technical requirements against a set of predefined criteria or constraints, and then arriving at an optimal design to achieve the expected results. These criteria, also known as design considerations, will be covered in the following subsections.

Coupling

Coupling refers to the degree of interdependency between the components or modules of a software system. *A good design is one that has low coupling.* In the context of API-led architectures, there will be multiple APIs and underlying subsystems involved in the solution. Low coupling will allow you to change or upgrade the components independently, without this impacting any other components in the system.

By focusing on building the components as atomic, self-contained parts, you can get optimal flexibility and improve your reusability. You can change or replace the components quite easily.

You can read more about the different types of coupling here: `https://www.geeksforgeeks.org/software-engineering-coupling-and-cohesion/`.

Chattiness

Chattiness refers to the number of calls the API consumer is required to make to get the necessary information. Chattiness must be avoided in your API design. Otherwise, it will lead to very poor end user experience. Multiple API calls consume both network bandwidth and increase the overall transaction time for any scenario.

API operations must be designed in a way that they provide the information or data that's been requested in one go. Transaction modeling techniques that use sequence diagrams can be adopted to identify whether there is chattiness in the workflow.

Chattiness is also considered to be a performance anti-pattern. Refer to this article to find out more: `https://docs.microsoft.com/en-us/azure/architecture/antipatterns/chatty-io/`.

Client complexity

The **clients** of an API refers to the variety of applications that connect and use the API to complete different business workflows and scenarios. All modern API interfaces must be designed to support a variety of clients, including devices, mobile phones, web browsers, desktop apps, and even service applications.

It must be noted that different constraints may apply as to how the clients behave and process API requests. For example, let's say a UI screen must display the list of orders that have been received. In a mobile app, only a subset of information may be necessary compared to a web client on a PC that has a larger form factor. So, it would be recommended to build APIs in such a fashion that the payload that's delivered is appropriate for the client.

This approach adds a bit of complexity to API design. However, the end result is more performant client apps.

Cognitive complexity

Cognitive complexity is a measure of the number of processes that are required to complete a specific task. In the context of an API operation, it refers to the number of functional blocks that must be traversed when the API is invoked.

Cognitive complexity impacts both the performance as well as the maintainability of an API. The more code or logic that you have in your API, the more difficult it will be to unit test all the paths, so any upgrades or changes are risky. There are tools such as **SonarQube** that can measure the cognitive complexity of your code.

In general, cognitive complexity must be low for a good API design. If there are multiple process steps, you should remodel your business workflow to avoid incurring high cognitive complexity in your components.

Caching

Caching refers to the ability to store copies of data that are not frequently updated using one of the following options:

- In memory, within the API layer itself
- In a low latency distributed store such as **Redis Cache**

Caching is frequently used for all static or reference data that does not change frequently. You can also cache transaction data, but that requires careful thinking. Cache invalidation technique must be deployed so that users don't receive stale information. Caching hugely improves the overall response time for the API.

For an API platform, caching helps with the following:

- Reducing the network traffic as the API doesn't always need to call other services or the database

- Improving the availability of the API

- Reducing server response time and latency

- Increasing throughput and scalability

Caching strategies must be carefully planned, especially when dealing with transactional data, as it impacts the *freshness* of data. Cache retention and purging strategies must also be planned to remove data from the cache before it becomes stale.

You can review the cache aside pattern that you plan to incorporate in your cloud APIs here: `https://docs.microsoft.com/en-us/azure/architecture/patterns/cache-aside`.

Response caching

This refers to the technique of storing copies of the response output of the API call either on the server, the browser, or the client making the API call. This allows for faster access to the data, thereby improving the overall responsiveness of the application.

The response data that's obtained from the endpoint is stored in the local cache with a specified a **time to live** (**TTL**), also known as the expiration window. For example, if the TTL is set to 300 seconds, then the client will make use of the data from the cache until the cache data becomes invalidated.

You can read more about this here: `https://restfulapi.net/caching/`.

Discoverability

Discoverability refers to the ease with which information about the list of APIs, their corresponding operations, and usage techniques can be accessed. This is only possible when you create sufficient documentation about the interface and data contracts. You should make use of the OpenAPI Specification to document your APIs. These specification files (in `yaml`/`json` format) are important to API management tools such as Azure API Management so that they are accessible to the developers consuming the API.

Note that API documentation is of paramount importance, especially for all public APIs. The adoption of the API platform is largely dependent on how easily developers can complete their integrations. Hence, you must provide as much information as possible in the definition files to avoid any ambiguity in understanding.

Versioning

APIs typically undergo multiple revisions as part of the change management cycles. Hence, it is imperative that you adopt a proper **versioning** strategy to distinctly identify what changed in which version. Furthermore, the changes must be backward compatible to ensure that any existing client integrations are not impacted.

Two types of changes can occur within an API, namely, *breaking* changes and *non-breaking* changes. You must create an upward major version when introducing breaking changes in your API.

So, what is a breaking change? You can consider the following scenarios as breaking changes:

- A change in the format (schema) of the response object; for example, adding new fields or elements, removing elements, changing the data types of elements, and so on

- A change in the format for request and response object types; for example, changing the definition of the data objects, adding or removing parameters expected by the API, and so on

- Deprecating or deleting the existing operations of the API

Non-breaking changes, such as adding a new endpoint (operations) to the API, can be treated as enhancements. We advise that you increment the major version for such cases as well, to efficiently track the revisions of your API.

Implementing versioning

API versioning can be implemented using one of the following techniques:

- **URI path based**: Appending the version information in the URI paths is the most straightforward method of API versioning.

  For example, the following two URLs represent separate versions of the quoting service API:

  ```
  https://api.packinsurance.com/quotingservice/v1
  https://api.packinsurance.com/quotingservice/v2
  ```

  You can append the versioning information in different ways when you're using a URI path-based approach.

- **Use a query string parameter**: By using a query string parameter (for example, `api-version`), you can differentiate between the versions. This is a common technique that's used in REST APIs as switching versions is easier than changing the actual URI paths.

  For example, the following two URLs represent separate versions of the quoting service API:

  ```
  https://api.packinsurance.com/quotingservice/
  getquote?api-version=1.0
  https://api.packinsurance.com/quotingservice/
  getquote?api-version=2.0
  ```

- **Versioning using the Accept header**: Sometimes, it is preferred to keep the URIs constant by differentiating between the versions using the information that's been sent by the client in the **Accept HTTP header**. This approach adds a little bit of complexity to your API controllers as you need to manage the additional processing logic of reading the header value and determining which content to send. Furthermore, the clients must know what value to send as part of the header while invoking the API.

  For example, the following header values indicate the different response outputs:

  ```
  Accept: application/quote.v1+json
  Accept: application/quote+json;version=2.0
  ```

- **Use a custom request header**: An alternative to using the Accept header is to make use of a custom header (for example, `accept-version` or something similar) to indicate the content version that's been requested.

For example, the following header values indicate different response outputs:

```
accept-version:v1
accept-version:v2
```

Although the technique of using custom headers adds flexibility and is simple to use, it's usually less preferred over the other approaches suggested here.

> **Note**
>
> For RESTful APIs, either the URI path-based or query string approaches are more preferred for API versioning over other approaches.

In the next section, we will review some of the recommended design practices that must be considered when building API-centric solutions.

Exploring recommended practices

The following list of recommended practices is a compilation of the *good habits* that development teams must embrace to be successful in their implementations. You may use this as a checklist for the purpose of training your project teams, or while conducting technical reviews. However, note that this list is not meant to serve as comprehensive guidance. There may be additional practices that you wish to consider based on your experience and research on this subject.

Design should adhere to the SOLID principles

Introduced in 2000 by Michael Feathers, and subsequently popularized by Robert C Martin, the SOLID principles are a set of five design principles that play a very important role in object-oriented design. These principles help create robust, scalable, and maintainable software architectures.

The term SOLID is an acronym that stands for the following:

- **S**: **Single Responsibility Principle (SRP)**
- **O**: **Open-Closed Principle (OCP)**
- **L**: **Liskov Substitute Principle (LSP)**
- **I**: **Interface Segregation Principle (ISP)**
- **D**: **Dependency Inversion Principle (ISP)**

You can read more about the SOLID principles here: `https://www.geeksforgeeks.org/solid-principle-in-programming-understand-with-real-life-examples/`.

You can download and read this whitepaper on how to use the Single Responsibility Principle for your cloud architectures in Azure here: `https://azure.microsoft.com/en-us/resources/cloud-solid-cloud-architecture-and-the-single-responsibility-principle/en-us/`.

> **Note**
>
> It is recommended that you evaluate your component designs by applying these principles to identify improvement areas. It requires a little bit of practice and discipline to get oriented in the right way before you can exploit the benefits offered by applying the five design principles.

The key benefits of using the SOLID principles in your design can be summarized as follows:

- Modular and loosely coupled services
- Highly testable components
- Maintainable and easily extendable design

Now, let's look at the design in terms of flexibility.

Design should be flexible to change

Your API designs should not be rigid or static. They should have the flexibility to change as the requirements change. It is suggested that you make use of strategies that allow more designs to be altered without significant maintenance costs.

Use the Decision Analysis and Resolution technique

Decision Analysis and Resolution (DAR), which originated as part of the CMMI process areas, is a very useful technique for recording important design decisions. Basically, DAR is a formal evaluation process in which you compare multiple viable alternatives against a predefined criterion. DAR provides a structure that ensures that any design decisions are scrutinized using a ranking model before a choice is made.

You can read more about DAR here: `https://www.software-quality-assurance.org/cmmi-decision-analysis-and-resolution.html`.

Often, technical teams tend to go with their past learnings, instead of making use of any recent advancements in technology. Using a DAR kind of approach is useful in broadening your thought processes when it comes to selecting the best possible choice.

Let's illustrate this with an example. When it comes to building microservices, there are multiple choices for the compute plane on Azure. This ranges from using App Service, to Kubernetes, and so on.

For simplicity, we will only consider five criteria and use a scale of 0 to 3 to indicate the advantage of using the respective service:

			Option 1	Option 2	Option 3
			App Service	Azure Kubernetes Services	Service Fabric
SL No	Criteria	Weightage			
1	Programming Language	3	2	3	1
2	Containerization	3	0	3	2
3	Enterprise Scale Architecture	3	0	3	3
4	Cloud Native	3	3	1	2
5	Community Support	2	2	3	1
		Weighted Sum	19	36	26

Figure 6.1 – Template for the Decision Analysis and Resolution technique

Thus, we can see that, as per the analysis we did previously, Azure Kubernetes Service appears to be the best choice.

> **A word of caution!**
>
> The output of DAR analysis is heavily influenced by the factors that are used for evaluation, the weights that are attached, and the preference rating that's applied. Hence, due diligence must be followed to avoid skewing the responses. It is better to provide justification using pros and cons analysis as well, to indicate why any particular choice is better compared to the other for any given given criteria.

DAR techniques are useful for conveying the basis of making any decisions, especially when you're presenting to a technical board during architecture/design review meetings. However, DAR should only be used for major design decisions, to avoid it becoming a bottleneck or churning out technical designs.

Produce documentation as per industry standards

With the emergence of public APIs driving innovation in the marketplace, there has been increased impetus on properly documenting all your API assets. API documentation describes the technical content of the API and how to integrate with it. Users and developers refer to this information to understand the products and services that are available. Hence, it is imperative that the content is produced in a professional manner to improve its adoption and usage.

Traditionally, developers don't pay much attention to documentation. However, this approach will not work anymore. API documentation must be treated like any other work product that must be produced with quality. Good API documentation is a piece of art. It should be consistent with the industry standards and must be treated as an enabler for your API platform.

Read this article to understand more about the importance of API documentation: `https://swagger.io/blog/api-documentation/what-is-api-documentation-and-why-it-matters/`.

Secure by design

We studied API security considerations from an architecture perspective in *Chapter 4, Assuring the Quality of the API Service (or Product)*. Hence, in this section, only the key points that apply to API design have been listed:

- **Implement authorization**:

    a) Protect HTTP methods: Each method or operation of the API must be protected appropriately, as per the authorization requirements.

    b) Whitelist allowable methods: Within your API, operations protect the code flow by validating the HTTP verbs that are used to access the API. Return error codes if the supported verbs are not part of the request to prevent malicious access.

    c) Protect privileged actions and sensitive resource collection: Apply role-based and attribute-based authorization checks to follow the principle of least privilege.

    d) Protect against **cross-site request forgery** (**CSRF**) (CSRF) Implement strategies to incorporate OWASP checks to prevent CSRF attacks.

- **Input validation**:

    a) URL validation: Ensure that all the possible inputs to your HTTP request, including URLs, query parameters, headers, and so on, have been validated.

    b) Validate incoming content types: Validate your incoming content types to ensure that clients only send valid content.

    c) Validate response types: Validate the data format in which the response that is sent to the client.

    d) XML input validation as applicable: Validate and securely parse any incoming XML data files as they can be susceptible to XML-based attacks.

- **Output encoding**:

    a) Security headers: Add the necessary headers while sending the response to the client so that the client (for example, the browser) can interpret the resource correctly.

    b) JSON/XML encoding: Use proper encoders and validators when working with JSON and XML data.

- **Cryptography**:

    a) Data in transit: Mandate the use of TLS for communication.

    b) Data in storage: When handling sensitive data, ensure that it is encrypted using modern and secure cryptography techniques.

    c) Message integrity: Make use of OAuth tokens in the request header to ensure the integrity of the transmission.

- **HTTP status codes**: Follow the standard conventions while defining the response code for your APIs. This is critical while building REST-type APIs.

Security is of paramount importance in any solution. The points listed here serve as a basic checklist that must be followed at a minimum. Based on your IT practices and their maturity, additional cyber security-related design guidelines may apply to your specific implementations.

Optimized for response time

We must design the components or parts that make up the API so that the response time is optimal. In *Chapter 4, Assuring the Quality of the API Service (or Product)*, we studied the concept of performance modeling, which is used to model the business flows and their expected performance, as measured through the response time. The response time of any API is impacted when under load. Hence, while designing an API, you must conduct analysis of the request flow path to identify the potential bottlenecks and then adjust your design to either eliminate these bottlenecks or optimize the internal calls.

Let's explain this with an example. Here, we have a client (say, a mobile app) that uses a CRUD API (microservice) hosted in the Azure cloud for various operations. The call flow from the client through the various components of the API is shown here:

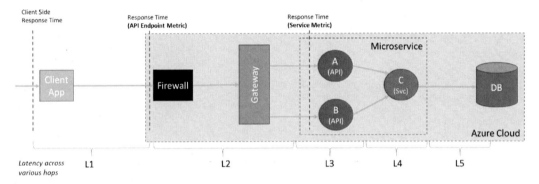

Figure 6.2 – Latency across various hops during an API operation

As we can see, there are various factors that contribute to the overall latency of an API operation that impact the client-side and server-side response times. If we analyze the request call flow, we will see a few things that will impact the overall client-side response time:

- L1 is impacted by the geolocation variance between the client and the firewall. For example, for services hosted in North America, users in Europe may experience some increased network latency compared to users accessing the API from North America.

- L2 is typically impacted by the scale of the firewall and gateway services. These are mostly pass-through shared services and should be designed for various load expectations.

- Within the microservice block, **Service C** acts as the **data access layer** (**DAL**). Hence, the scale and latency of C (L4) will have an impact on the API response metric. It must be analyzed whetherit benefits from referencing the DAL as a shared library instead of hosting it as a separate microservice. Note that any out-of-process calls will add to the overall throughput and latency.

- The database latency (L5) will have an additional impact on the overall response time. Hence, all the queries and transactions must perform faster.

Thus, by analyzing the various latency factors, the design can be adjusted so that an optimal API response time is achieved.

API testing

The goal of API testing, which can be achieved through manual or automated tests, is centered around determining whether the API meets the expectations of functionality, reliability, performance, and security. Project teams should focus on automating the API tests. This investment pays off in the long term. These API tests can be integrated as part of the CI/CD processes that verify the quality of the changes being deployed.

Testing types

Let's understand this by reviewing the important types of API tests that can be implemented:

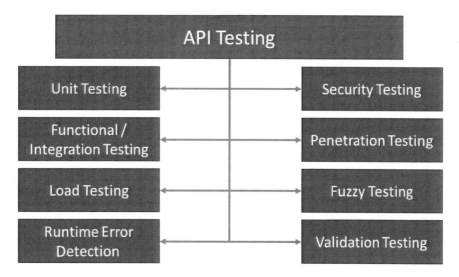

Figure 6.3 – API testing categorization

Each of these categories will be explained in the following subsections.

Unit testing

This the most common type of testing that happens on any software solution. Basically, the developer writes automated tests to verify the functionality of the unit of code (typically, a function or a class) that they have written for the solution.

The objective of unit testing is to verify the different code paths for their completeness and to detect any logic-related errors. Unit tests must be maintained as requirements change. Hence, investing in unit testing is ongoing as more code modules are implemented. However, these tests are extremely useful for detecting any build breaks due to bug fixes or enhancements being rolled out.

Functional or integration testing

Functional testing, also known as integration testing, aims to verify the business functionality or behavior that's implemented by the API. Functional testing focuses on verifying the different functions and their associated business rules, including data validation.

Functional testing is accomplished by specifying a set of input parameters for the function, as per the interface definition, and then checking the response that's obtained against the expected result. This is called integration testing as it requires the API to be fully deployed in an environment with all the other working components, including active connections to the database.

Functional testing is extremely useful for verifying the quality of the solution. Teams that have high agility in their release cycles invest heavily in writing automated functional tests that are integrated with the CI/CD pipelines. Basically, every code change can be deployed to an integration testing environment, and then the automated suite of applicable functional tests can be run to verify whether there are any regression issues. Otherwise, the build can be promoted to production. This drastically reduces the verification cycle time, thereby improving the cycle time of the releases.

Load testing

The goal of load testing is to verify the scalability of the API when it's subject to a significant number of concurrent requests (for example, 1K/10K/100K requests) hitting the API. Load testing is conducted to understand the performance of the API under normal and peak load situations. The test results are compared against the predicted performance models to identify issues that require further API tuning.

Security testing

Security testing is conducted as part of the API life cycle to verify whether the software meets the security requirements. Security testing may also involve code inspections to verify the usage of encryption/decryption techniques, validate authentication and authorization checks, and check whether all the components follow *secure by design* principles. Security testing also involves static analysis involving various code analyzers to detect OWASP and other design-related issues.

Penetration testing

Penetration testing is an extension of security testing, which is conducted to detect whether any security vulnerabilities exist in the solution that can be easily exploited by an attacker. These tests are performed in such a way that they mimic the scenario of a hacker trying to force access to the system by exploiting a loophole. Considering the increased rate of cyber security attacks, these tests have become very important in preventing any denial-of-service attacks.

Penetration testing often requires specialized knowledge and tools. Hence, project teams must identify this as a crucial dependency during their planning cycle.

Fuzzy testing

Fuzzy testing involves passing a lot of random data to the API and verifying whether it can gracefully handle erroneous inputs. Through fuzzy testing, you can verify whether the API is handling the exception flows properly.

Runtime error detection

These types of tests involve testing the runtime operation of the API. They are useful in detecting error conditions, resource leaks, unnecessary locks, and other monitoring-related events. They are useful for optimizing the code of the API.

Validation testing

Validation testing is done at the end of the development life cycle. Its core objective is to verify the following:

- **Product**: Whether the API meets the requirements of the product
- **Behavior**: Whether the API is operating correctly with the various datasets and produces the expected results
- **Efficiency**: Whether the API is functioning in the most optimized way

The answers to these questions help the project teams identify whether the API can accomplish the business objectives against the established standards and guidelines.

Benefits of API testing

Having the ability to test and verify your services independently, without actual consumers, significantly improves the chances of detecting any faults that may impact the quality of the service before they are reported by users. This provides greater predictability and confidence to the team that is building and managing the API services.

A few important benefits of API testing are as follows:

- Detect integration issues/bugs early in the life cycle, without requiring the actual UI application to be fully developed.

- Functionality breaks due to fixes or enhancements being introduced can be detected easily.

- Security threats and vulnerabilities are detected and mitigated.

- Ensure adherence to SLOs/SLAs, as per the commitment of the service provider.

- Improve the monitoring, auditing, and alerting capabilities that are implemented in the solution.

- Reduce technical debt and ensure the quality of the product.

Size and granularity

When developing API interfaces, project teams are often challenged with the decision to identify the right level of granularity. While DDD techniques do allow you to identify the different microservices that are required, clarity may be lacking regarding the definitions for the actual physical services that must be developed.

When it comes to designing the actual physical API interfaces or controllers, there are five options to choose from: monoliths, macroservices, miniservices, microservices, and nanoservices (or functions). Let's have a quick look at each:

- **Monoliths**: In this approach, while the code may be modular, the entire business functionality will be contained in a single physical deployment unit. Most legacy systems follow this kind of design and are difficult to upgrade and maintain.

- **Macroservices**: In this approach, there may be multiple service domains or business processes that are interdependent on each other, and they will be contained within a single service. There is a thin line of difference between monoliths and macroservices, and it's up to the discipline of the development teams that the right level of granularity is ensured.

- **Miniservices**: In this approach, the code for a single business domain will be contained within a single service. Typically, they tend to grow as new functionality gets introduced.

- **Microservices**: This is the most preferred choice for modern cloud-based development. Here, any specific business domain is broken down into logical units of abstraction that can be independently deployed and scaled.

- **Nanoservices or functions**: This is another extreme end of the spectrum, where every individual function can be independently deployed and scaled. This approach finds usage in some use cases such as large event processing, IoT, and big data pipelines.

> **Business microservices versus API services**
>
> A business microservice is a logical grouping of one or many physical API services. For example, in the previous chapters, for the Packt Insurance scenario, we depicted how the Quote microservice is comprised of two to three separate physical services. For simplicity, the terms microservice and API service have been used interchangeably in this chapter. They both mean the same thing; that is, a single physical deployable service.

Too much granularity adds operations and management overhead, whereas large services are difficult to maintain and upgrade. Hence, you must apply the following key considerations to arrive at the right level of service granularity:

- Release agility expected.

- Separate hosting and scaling to meet variable usage loads.

- Use different API styles for different purposes.

- Operational cost.

Service granularity is the most important concern for all application developers. Hence, defaulting to coarser-grained (for example, microservices) is more preferred for all scenarios, followed by identifying a limited set of scenarios that will benefit from finer-grained (for example, nanoservices) services.

Content negotiation

Content negotiation refers to the ability of the API to provide different representations of a resource, depending on what the client has requested. For example, a data object can be represented in XML, JSON, or even plain text. So, when using the content negotiation feature, the API can return the same data but in different formats.

Content negotiation can be server-driven or agent-driven:

- **Server-driven**: The decision to identify the best representation of content is made by the server by using an algorithm or logic.

- **Agent-driven**: The client of the API explicitly asks on the format that it expects the response to be provided in. To achieve this, the client uses either an HTTP request header (for example, Content-Type) or calls a different resource URI to specify the resource format. This is relatively simple to implement on the server side.

You can read more about content negotiation here: `https://restfulapi.net/content-negotiation/`.

Prefer stateless over stateful services

API services can be both stateful as well as stateless. However, stateless services are preferred over stateful due to their obvious benefits. First, let's understand the difference between the two:

- **Stateful services**: This service stores or maintains state information on the server it runs. Basically, the state of the data is persisted either *in memory* or within a caching tier that can be externalized. The stateful service still may have a backend database but for the clients, most of the information is served from the cache. Stateful services are useful in certain scenarios. Since the data is close to the compute, it speeds up requests being processed.

- **Stateless services**: This type of service does not store any data on the server. It processes all incoming requests by interacting directly with the backend database. It can externalize information that's stored in the cache stores of the client. For example, when the API is invoked by a web browser, the data can be saved to the local cache storage of the browser.

Stateless services are beneficial due to the following reasons:

- Easy to scale to meet the load and availability requirements.

- Simpler to revise and upgrade as there is no fear of any data getting lost.

- Data is always in a consistent state as it is stored in the database.

User-digestible response codes and messages

One common mistake all developers make is assuming that API consumers are tech-savvy people who will understand the technical jargon easily. However, this is not always true, so the response codes and messages that are returned by the API must be easy to understand and follow certain predefined, commonly used standards.

For example, when an API consumer invokes an API passing invalid data, then the API must return a user-friendly message stating what the problem was with the data. This will make it meaningful for the developers so that they take action to fix the data payload in order to successfully complete the operation.

API response codes and messages must be properly documented as part of the API definition and periodically revised to improve the experience of the users.

Using cloud design patterns

Azure Architecture Center has published a collection of cloud design patterns that development teams must plan to incorporate in their designs.

You can review the full catalog of cloud design patterns here: `https://docs.microsoft.com/en-us/azure/architecture/patterns/`.

These patterns are mostly structural and behavioral patterns that address common challenges for cloud-based applications.

Projects teams must prioritize and plan to use one or more patterns for their respective services as they have been tried and tested in various customer scenarios.

In the next few sections, we will cover some of the modern implementation patterns that are used while building microservice-based API solutions.

Implementing an API service using design patterns

It is recommended that you make use of the microservices architecture and its associated design patterns to implement cloud-based enterprise API-centric solutions. You can find a rich catalog of such design patterns here: `https://microservices.io/`.

In this section, we will cover the most used structural and behavioral patterns, study their pros and cons, and share some usage scenarios as well. All the finer, more granular details of each pattern will not be covered in this book. You can explore the *Further reading* section to learn more about the respective patterns. These patterns target commonly faced design challenges and can be easily reused in your respective scenarios. Having a good grasp of the usage of these patterns is essential to building great API architectures.

> **Good read**
>
> There are a lot of reference materials available on microservices that offer insightful and prescriptive guidance on this topic. One such useful reference is *eShop on Containers*, which is available at `https://github.com/ dotnet-architecture/eShopOnContainers`. You will find a lot of reference code and other ideas for your microservices design strategies here.

In the following sections, we will review the five most commonly used implementation patterns.

Data-driven CRUD API

A data-driven CRUD API is the most simplistic representation of a microservice. It is commonly used in scenarios wherein there is less complexity in the way the domain model entity objects are accessed or updated. The following diagram shows what a simple CRUD API looks like:

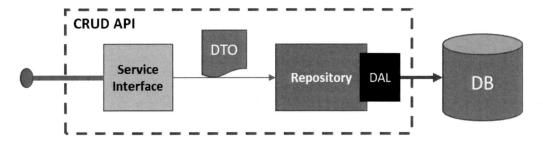

Figure 6.4 – A simple CRUD API

This pattern behaves like a *layered architecture*, but all the code components are deployed together in a single microservice. Also, there is no business layer in this type of API.

A **data transfer object** (**DTO**) may be used as the published data model for exchanging information with the consumers of this API. A CRUD API may implement caching strategies to improve the response time for the read operations.

Let's study the pros and cons and typical usage scenarios of a data-driven CRUD API pattern. The key benefits of this pattern are as follows:

- Used for building data services that do not have any business logic
- Low complexity due to its simple design

A few of the constraints while using this pattern are as follows:

- Requires data caching strategies to improve the performance of the read operations.
- The complexity of the implementation requires highly skilled developers.
- Used only for fine-grained services with simple entity schemas.

Some common uses of this pattern are as follows:

- For implementing reference or master data services. These APIs are typically lightweight and involve a limited set of entities.
- Shared data services that will be accessed by other microservices in the solution.

Command and Query Responsibility Segregation (CQRS)

Command and Query Responsibility Segregation (**CQRS**) is a software design pattern that separates the code or components into two parts: one that reads the state and another that modifies the state.

In other words, the application provides APIs that do the following:

- Accept `command` messages to update the data.
- Provide separate `query` interfaces to read the persisted data.

You can read more about the CQRS pattern here: `https://docs.microsoft.com/en-us/azure/architecture/patterns/cqrs`.

A very simplified version of the CQRS pattern, with separate command and query interfaces, is depicted here:

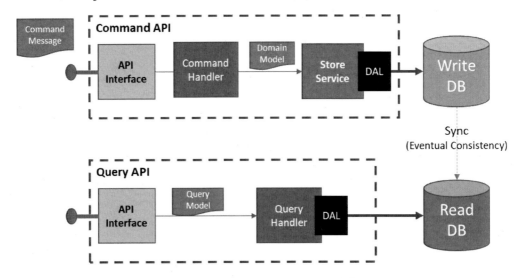

Figure 6.5 – CQRS pattern using separate API services

The most common usage of CQRS is for implementing *domain-driven design* behaviors through APIs. Using this approach, the Read operations can be isolated from the Create, Update, and Delete operations. The code components can be logically separated within a single API, or even physically by creating separate API endpoints. This approach is extremely useful in scenarios wherein the volume of read requests may be significantly higher than write requests or vice versa. Physical separation allows the components to be scaled independently of each other.

> **Note**
> CQRS is often used in conjunction with the Event Sourcing pattern. In this case, the write database can implement a message store that receives the incoming command messages that are to be processed.

Let's study the pros and cons and typical usage scenarios of the CQRS pattern.

The key benefits of this pattern are as follows:

- Commonly used for **Domain Driven Design (DDD)** behaviors.
- Allows read and write operations to be scaled independently from each other.
- Used in scenarios that require high availability of data (read operations).
- Good adherence to REST principles.

A few of the constraints while using this pattern are as follows:

- Requires data consistency to be handled between write and read stores.

- There may be a learning curve for project teams not familiar with DDD techniques.

- The complexity of the implementation requires highly skilled developers.

Some common uses of this pattern are as as follows:

- For building highly scalable microservices

- For implementing DDD behaviors

Event Store API (Event Sourcing)

The Event Store API, also known as the **Event Sourcing** pattern, is used in asynchronous event-based messaging scenarios. Here, the state changes that are made to an entity are represented as events that are saved to a transient event store, instead of them being used to directly update the actual entity. The actual state of the entity is derived by sequentially processing all the corresponding stored events on that *entity*.

The following diagram is a representation of the Event Store API:

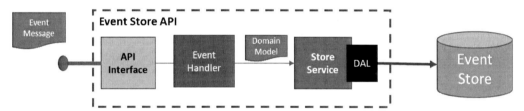

Figure 6.6 – Event Store API

The Event Store pattern is often used in conjunction with CQRS. This pattern provides very high throughput for write operations.

You can read more about this here: `https://docs.microsoft.com/en-us/azure/architecture/patterns/event-sourcing`.

Let's study the pros and cons and typical usage scenarios of the Event Store API pattern.

The key benefits of this pattern are as follows:

- Used for building highly scalable, loosely coupled systems.

- Each state change is considered an atomic transaction.

- Events are stored in a chronological manner, making it easier to track their history.

- Wide application of event-driven architectures in everyday business scenarios.

A few of the constraints while using this pattern are as follows:

- Works in conjunction with the CQRS pattern to provide full functionality for a business domain entity.

- The overall complexity can be high, depending on the nature of the business domain.

- Must support compensating transactions to handle missing events.

- The schema may have to be generalized for all entity types.

Some common uses of this pattern are as follows:

- Highly scalable transactional systems that use the asynchronous messaging pattern

- Event-driven architectures

Clean architecture

This is another very popular architecture style that is quite powerful while building data-oriented API microservices. The clean architecture was introduced by Robert C. Martin, also popularly known as Uncle Bob. He presented the basic concepts of this pattern in the following article: `https://blog.cleancoder.com/uncle-bob/2012/08/13/the-clean-architecture.html`.

For an API microservice, the clean architecture can be visualized as follows:

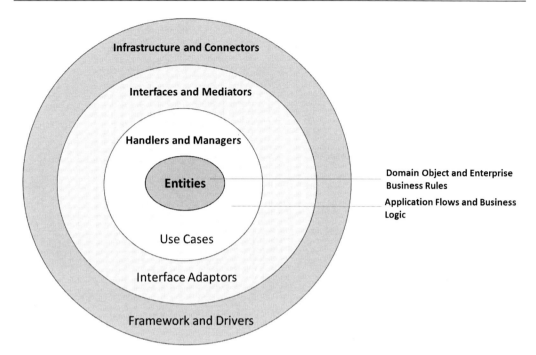

Figure 6.7 – API design using the clean architecture

The central theme of the clean architecture is the principle of decomposing your system into layers that have distinct and well-defined roles. The different layers in the architecture can be summarized as follows:

- **Entities**: This layer, called the *domain layer*, represents the domain models (or entities) and the enterprise business rules that apply to it. The domain models and rules are universal to its usage and do not change based on the various interactions. They control what validations apply to the data before being stored in the persistent store.

- **Use Cases**: This layer, called the *application layer*, represents the various application flows and business logic that operate on these entities. For an API service, typically, the handler and manager components participate in executing the various business functionalities.

- **Interface Adaptors**: This layer serves as the main interaction touchpoint between the application layer and its interaction with the external world, such as a database or user interface.

- **Framework and Drivers**: This layer represents the framework and infrastructure components that participate in the flow of information in and out of the system.

You can find an example of how to use this pattern in the following GitHub repository: `https://github.com/mattia-battiston/clean-architecture-example`.

There are derivatives of the clean architecture, namely the **onion architecture** and the **hexagonal architecture**. These are basically implementations of the key concepts presented in the *clean architecture*. The core objective of all these variations is *testability* and *separation of concerns*. The clear isolation between the layers allows us to reduce the dependencies, thereby allowing any specific layer change to be implemented independently of the others. The layer that is most important and stable will be the domain model.

Let's study the pros and cons and typical usage scenarios of the clean architecture pattern.

The key benefits of this pattern are as follows:

- Improves testability of code.
- Independent from the database.
- All the business logic is constrained within the use case layer.
- Can be easily applied to most types of business domains.

A few of the constraints while using this pattern are as follows:

- Code blocks may be duplicated across layers.
- Implementation warrants discipline and practice.

Some common uses of this pattern are as follows:

- API services involving complex business domains with multiple workflows
- Synchronous HTTP API services that make use of additional patterns such as Aggregator, Saga, and so on
- Alternative to CQRS to keep complexity low

Backends for Frontends (BFF)

The **Backends for Frontends** (BFF) pattern operates on the principle of creating separate backend services for separate frontend applications or channel interfaces. This technique is preferred when the actual backend service containing the domain logic and other rules must not change based on the UI interfaces. This pattern introduces a wrapper layer on top of the actual backend service. These lightweight wrapper services act as backends for the respective frontends handling communication and interaction with the underlying data service:

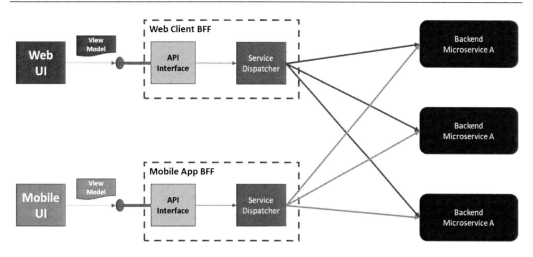

Figure 6.8 – BFF pattern

You can read more about the BFF pattern here: `https://docs.microsoft.com/`
`en-us/azure/architecture/patterns/backends-for-frontends`.

Let's study the pros and cons and typical usage scenarios of the BFF pattern.

The key benefits of this pattern are as follows:

- Enhances the experience based on the client

- Better security and control over the channels

- Also acts as an aggregator, removing chattiness between the UI and backend services

A few of the constraints while using this pattern are as follows:

- High maintainability due to code duplication among BFFs.

- Increase in deployment complexity if more frontend applications are used.

- Requires discipline for strict adherence to the BFF pattern. The APIs are mostly passthrough ones and don't have any business logic.

Some common uses of this pattern are as follows:

- As a backend for responsive or adaptive UI applications

- Implementing micro frontends-based architectures

- Additional security layer between the UI layer and the actual domain services

> **Other patterns**
>
> Depending on your business requirements, you may wish to make use of various other design patterns for your entire microservices architecture, such as Aggregator, Saga, Proxy, Chaining, Strangler, Branching, and so on. It is suggested that you review them using the references provided at the end of this chapter.

In the next section, we will take a brief look at a few of the most important tools that are currently available to the developer community while building API-centric solutions.

Developer toolbox

As an API developer, you must improve your awareness and master your skills on using a variety of tools that will aid in implementing, testing, and even debugging and troubleshooting production issues. In this section, we have provided references to a few commonly used tools while developing applications for the Azure cloud:

- **Visual Studio Code**: Visual Studio Code is a free code editor from Microsoft that allows you to quickly develop, build, deploy, and test your modern cloud applications. It can be used on Windows, Linux, and macOS. It has built-in support for a wide range of programming languages. It also has a community of widgets and plugins that will immensely improve your productivity.

  If you are a developer, you must try out Visual Studio Code. Visit this link to find out more: `https://code.visualstudio.com/`.

- **Swagger.io**: This is another very useful productivity tool that aims to simplify your API development process. You can quickly design your APIs with robust documentation that's created as per the OpenAPI Specification v3. The open source tools come bundled with rich visual editors that are quite intuitive and easy to use, thereby simplifying the whole design experience.

  Find out more here: `https://swagger.io/`.

- **Postman**: Collaborate with your teams while you develop amazing APIs. Postman is a robust API testing tool. It provides a visual interface to simulate the HTTP request. You can create workspaces and share them with your teams.

  Postman is the tool for your API-first development needs. Find out more here: `https://www.postman.com/use-cases/api-first-development/`.

- **DAPR.io**: DAPR is a framework for building highly resilient event-driven microservices.

  Find out more here: `https://dapr.io/`.

- **K6.io**: This is a powerful open source load testing framework that can be easily integrated as part of your CI/CD processes. With the K6 JavaScript-based framework, you can quickly create tests that simulate user load scenarios. It also comes with a CLI version. This is very useful during the development stages for measuring response times and detecting any performance bottlenecks with your APIs.

  Learn more about K6.io here: `https://k6.io`.

- **Apache JMeter**™: Apache JMeter™ is a Java-based open source tool that is quite popular for both functional testing and load testing. It is the most used tool for API performance testing. It has a friendly UI, can run on any platform, and offers very rich reporting capabilities to visualize the test results.

  You can find out more about JMeter here: `https://jmeter.apache.org/`.

- **Telerik Fiddler**: Fiddler is another very useful web debugging tool. It captures the network traffic between your computer and the internet. This tool is very useful in inspecting both incoming and outgoing traffic to visualize what's happening with HTTP requests. It can be used to replay any specific transactions to debug and isolate issues.

  You can find out more about Fiddler here: `https://www.telerik.com/fiddler`.

- **jwt.ms**: If you are using JSON Web Tokens (also known as OAuth tokens), then jwt.ms is the tool to use to view the claims that are part of the token. It has a simple UI that decodes your token and displays the list of claims contained in it, along with an explanation of the type of claim.

  Start decoding your JSON Web Tokens by visiting this: `https://jwt.ms/`.

- **Azure Application Insights**: You can bake in support for rich telemetry capture in all your API applications using Azure Application Insights. Use the logs to derive insights and detect performance issues, diagnose common errors, visualize an HTTP request using the end-to-end transaction flow, and collect metrics to derive various other metrics.

  Find out more about Azure Application Insights here: `https://docs.microsoft.com/en-us/azure/azure-monitor/app/app-insights-overview`.

The tools listed in this section are just an initial set that you must be familiar with. However, based on your choice of technology and platform, you may want to explore other tools that are frequently used by the community.

Summary

In this chapter, we reviewed some important design -related aspects to consider while building API solutions. We also studied some of the recommended practices that can be easily used by development teams as a design checklist. Great API design requires discipline and constant attention to detail. By now, you must be familiar with the most common architectural patterns for implementing API-based microservices solutions. You should further explore the references and examples shared, so that you feel more confident while approaching your microservices designs in the future.

The practices and patterns discussed in this chapter are only a starting point. Building modern, API-centric solutions on the cloud requires a good balance between technical strategy and business workflows. You must experiment with DDD practices and use techniques such as **Event Storming** to model your domains more accurately, as well as to identify the various API microservices required for your solution.

In the next chapter, we will explore the importance of having the right DevOps practices in place for your API platform life cycle processes.

Further reading

- API Design Best Practices for Azure: `https://docs.microsoft.com/en-us/azure/architecture/best-practices/api-design`
- API Design Best Practices and Design Principles: `https://tutorialspedia.com/api-design-best-practices-and-design-principles/`
- 16 REST API Design Best Practices and Guidelines: `https://searchapparchitecture.techtarget.com/tip/16-REST-API-design-best-practices-and-guidelines`
- API Testing: `https://docs.katalon.com/katalon-studio/docs/introduction_api_testing.html`
- 9 Types of API Tests: `https://nordicapis.com/9-types-of-tests-to-perform-on-your-apis/`
- Microservices Archtecture
- Microservice Granularity: `http://www.opengroup.org/soa/source-book/msawp/p6.htm`
- How Granular Should My Microservices Be?: `https://tcblog.protiviti.com/2019/09/04/moving-to-microservices-how-granular-should-my-services-be/`
- Design Stateless Services: `https://restfulapi.net/statelessness/`

- Checklist on Designing, Testing, and Releasing Your APIs: `https://mathieu.fenniak.net/the-api-checklist/`

- Top 5 Security Considerations for APIs: `https://blog.restcase.com/top-5-rest-api-security-guidelines/`

- Design Patterns for Microservices Architecture: `https://www.lambdatest.com/blog/design-patterns-for-micro-service-architecture/`

- The Six Most Common Microservices Architecture Design Patterns: `https://medium.com/analytics-vidhya/the-six-most-common-microservice-architecture-design-pattern-1038299dc396`

- A Quick Introduction to Clean Architecture: `https://www.freecodecamp.org/news/a-quick-introduction-to-clean-architecture-990c014448d2/`

- CQRS Translated into Clean Architecture: `https://blog.fals.io/2018-09-19-cqrs-clean-architecture/`

- Microservices Design Patterns: `http://web.archive.org/web/20190705163602/http:/blog.arungupta.me/microservice-design-patterns/`

- Java Design Patterns: `https://java-design-patterns.com/patterns/`

7
Accelerating through DevOps Essentials

DevOps as a buzzword has been doing rounds in all enterprises for quite some time now. IT leaders are busy figuring out what strategies and training are required to make the paradigm shift within their development teams. While there are many definitions for the term DevOps, the common theme that emerges across all of them is the fact that if you haven't started on your journey yet, then you must act now with a sense of urgency.

Organizations understand that their digital transformation will not be complete without an overhaul of their DevOps practices. For the short term, they focus on the key essentials that will meet their immediate business needs. For the longer term, they have to plan for more increased DevOps adoption to improve their IT maturity and **Software Development Life Cycle** (**SDLC**) practices followed across the various teams.

The purpose of this chapter is to focus on the importance of DevOps adoption within an enterprise and how to get it right. SDLC practices have a tight bearing on the business outcomes and making the culture shift at the right time can improve the overall maturity of the enterprise. We will understand the practices through the lens of how they bring value as measured through the various metrics of DevOps maturity.

In this chapter, we are going to cover the following main topics:

- Business objectives and key results
- The DevOps Dojo framework
- DevOps metrics and their importance
- Identifying the maturity index for your enterprise
- The power of GitHub and Azure DevOps
- DevOps in practice
- Tracking DevOps initiatives in backlog

We will make use of the DevOps Dojo White Belt foundation framework introduced by Microsoft to structure the recommendations provided in this chapter.

By the end of this chapter, you will understand how to prioritize your initiatives revolving around the various pillars and practices of DevOps to establish a modern process, thereby blurring the line between development and operations teams.

> **Food for thought**
>
> What is the DevOps maturity level of your organization? How do you measure the success of your DevOps practices?

Business objectives and key results

As we have understood in the previous chapters, enterprise initiatives are usually prioritized based on the business outcomes – some of them are immediate while others are more long-term. Hence, it is important to study the typical **Objectives and Key Results Objectives and Key Results (OKRs)** that may apply to any enterprise context and how they map to the various DevOps practices that must be implemented by the development teams.

Some of the important objectives and key results are as follows:

Objective	Key Results
Faster time to market	Deployment frequency: Every week
	Deployment time: <= 4 hours
	Lead time (major releases): Once every quarter
Increase the business value realized while maintaining or reducing costs	CI/CD processes: 100% automated
	Resource utilization (95th percentile): 80%
	Dashboards for monitoring both health and costs
Predictable and quality delivery, faster correction with fewer defects	High availability: > 99.9%
	RTO: < 1 hour, RPO: < 15 mins
Better processes across IT, automation, teamwork, and culture	MTTR: < 1 hour
	Lead time (bugs): < 8 hour
	Scaled Agile: feature teams: > 5
	Technical debt: < 1 week
Improved customer engagement and ability to quickly respond to market demands	CSAT: 4 or above
	Product planning: 50% of backlog focuses on customer feedback

In the next section, we will explore the DevOps Dojo framework introduced by Microsoft to evaluate how the OKRs map to the various capabilities.

The DevOps Dojo framework

In 2020, Microsoft introduced the DevOps Dojo White Belt framework, grouping the most important foundational practices into four pillars and eight capabilities, as shown here:

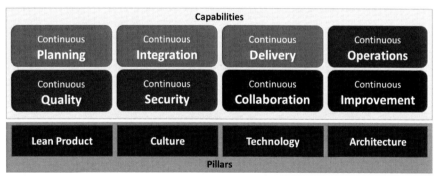

Figure 7.1 – DevOps Dojo White Belt foundation capabilities and pillars

You can read more about the DevOps Dojo White Belt foundation here: `https://docs.microsoft.com/en-us/learn/paths/devops-dojo-white-belt-foundation/`.

Each capability area and pillar is briefly described here:

Capability/Pillar	Description
Continuous Planning	Continuous planning is a practice that requires the various agile feature teams to come together and create an integrated plan capturing dependencies and sequencing of activities that are revised continuously on an ongoing basis. These plans are periodically revised based on stakeholder feedback, new feature requests based on market demand, and changes due to a shift in business priorities. The team uses Kanban boards or other mechanisms to track the identified work and their corresponding tasks that will be executed by the various team members.
Continuous Integration	**Continuous Integration (CI)** is a software development practice where the members of a development team publish their work outputs (for example, code files) to a central repository to integrate with the overall stable code of the solution. Automated builds are run on the code base to detect any integration issues or failures that may impact the quality of the code. CI can happen many times in a day.
Continuous Delivery	**Continuous Delivery (CD)** is a software development approach in which teams produce build outputs in short cycles, which is then subject to deployment validation and testing in an automated way. The purpose is to verify the quality of the build before it is released to production. CD practices help reduce the lead time and risk of releasing the software to production by keeping the count of changes to a very limited set.
Continuous Operations	Continuous operations is the ability to deliver uninterrupted service to the various users of the system through a good monitoring and alerting strategy. The objective is to minimize downtime by taking immediate action on any incidents.
Continuous Quality	Continuous quality is about fostering a quality culture and ensuring that teams are creating a superior user experience, building features that fit the market's timing, and enabling the characteristics of an application that deliver value faster than they create technical debt.
Continuous Security	Continuous security is a practice that detects any security concerns as part of the life cycle stages and proactively mitigates any risks through the adoption of control measures by the project teams. Continuous security in DevOps should cover a holistic view of security including secure architecture, governance, risk and compliance, app security, data security, infra security, secure operations, identity and access, and endpoint security.
Continuous Collaboration	Continuous collaboration is the ability to work together as a team of diverse individuals with different skills and role descriptions. The team makes use of available tools for collaboration, thereby demonstrating greater productivity and coordination.
Continuous Improvement	Continuous improvement is the ability for the team to measure the success of DevOps practices, and constantly revise them based on feedback from the various stakeholders.
Lean Product	The pillar of Lean Product lays emphasis on building software as products instead of short-lived projects.
Culture	Having the right culture within the team toward DevOps practices is essential to its adoption and success. It's all about mindset and having the right focus can drive the right outcomes.
Technology	Technology focuses on the importance of using the right set of tools (namely GitHub and Azure DevOps) to implement the DevOps processes end to end.
Architecture	Architecture must focus on the quality attributes of the solution.

We have selected the DevOps Dojo model for the discussion of the topics in this chapter as it is quite easy to remember and use. While the practices listed in the White Belt foundation are only a starting point, enterprises can extend on the concepts and identify additional practices that may be relevant for their context.

An important point to note would be that if you are planning to be a digital business, then streamlined DevOps processes should be part of your DNA. Otherwise, it will be quite difficult to accomplish the business objectives (as defined earlier in the *Business objectives and key results* section) that may be critical for the survivability of your business. We shall take a detailed look into each of these capabilities in the *DevOps in practice* section of this chapter.

Let's first understand the important benefits of having a good DevOps strategy.

The benefits of having a good DevOps strategy

The key business benefits that will be realized using this comprehensive DevOps strategy can be easily summarized as follows:

- Reduce lead time for releases from months to weeks.
- Increase the pace of delivering innovation/new capabilities to end users.
- Reduce the risk of detecting quality issues in production.
- Improve reliability of the production solution and recover from unplanned outages fast with minimal or no business impact.

Enterprises today may already have implemented different practices or be in the process of achieving them. Hence, it will be useful to assess your current maturity level to establish a baseline on your current maturity level. In the next section, we shall discuss, how you can use the framework to depict your maturity model.

DevOps metrics and their importance

There are a lot of different metrics that can be tracked by the development teams, to determine the maturity level of the DevOps practices and standards followed. These metrics help to identify issues or focus areas that must be investigated upon. They also provide feedback to ascertain the degree of business impact based on the priorities established for the team. Some would require immediate attention, while others will have to be planned.

Refer to this link to understand the comprehensive list of DevOps metrics as suggested by Gartner: `https://www.gartner.com/en/documents/3760663/data-driven-devops-use-metrics-to-guide-your-journey`.

In this chapter, we shall focus on nine of the most important metrics that are quite common and relevant while building API-centric solutions. They are as follows:

- **Deployment frequency**: This measures how frequently and with ease you can deploy software into production. Gone are the days when teams would follow a waterfall kind of approach and deploy something at say the end of 6-8 months. Businesses want greater agility today, and they want to release features in more of an iterative manner but at great speed. Teams should be able to deploy multiple times a day or even a week, if possible, without breaking anything.

- **Lead time**: Lead time typically refers to the overall duration it takes from the time the business needs/requirement is identified to the time it is finally deployed and is in use in production environments. Lead times are highly dependent on how efficient your SDLC process is and how well you manage your backlog and prioritize them. This metric is very crucial for start-ups as they would like to release new capabilities at a faster pace than other conventional businesses.

- **Deployment time**: Deployment time is the measure of how long it takes to deploy or upgrade an existing solution. Deployment time is impacted by the degree of automation in place for both installation and subsequent testing as needed. Manual processes, if any, must be eliminated, as they are both time-consuming and error-prone.

- **Code quality**: Code quality refers to a combination of metrics that determine the overall quality of the code that is being produced by the teams. The code quality index has a direct bearing on the technical debt of the solution. Code quality is typically measured using static code analyzers and other tools to detect issues or bugs in the code. Most of the static rules focus on identifying issues related to the usage of coding standards, design, code maintainability, performance, security, and other language-specific improvements. It can be further augmented by periodic manual inspections using a checklist on coding standards. The team should monitor code quality consistently and keep it within the acceptable thresholds. Many teams periodically prioritize fixing the technical debt over building new business functionality.

- **Automated test percentage**: Automated testing is a measure of the degree of automated tests that can be run during every release to certify the quality of the change. This includes all types of testing, such as unit, functional, integration, performance, and even security testing. These automated tests can quickly determine whether the change introduced can significantly impact a deployed service. This metric is always in discussion as it takes a significant investment of time for the automation to be robust and useful. For API platforms, this is a must-have metric.

- **Change failure rate**: Change failure rate refers to the ratio of the count of failed releases to the total releases done. It is reflecting on how many releases impacted the solution, something that requires proper **root cause analysis** (**RCA**) to avoid similar mistakes in the future. Release failures can happen due to multiple reasons. A few of them could be due to people issues (mistakes made by the DevOps team), but many others could be due to environmental factors as well. It is important to follow a structured RCA process to avoid repeating mistakes.

- **Mean time to recovery** (**MTTR**): MTTR refers to the duration it takes for a service to recover from the initial reported incident or detection of failure to the getting back into a proper healthy state. Outages in a production environment will disrupt the rhythm of the business, leading to huge financial and credibility losses. MTTR should be measured and controlled by using strategies to avoid downtime or availability issues.

- **Customer Tickets**: The adoption of any solution is largely dependent on the ease with which users can make use of the solution. The count of support tickets is also a measure of how good the solution is. A high count indicates the solution deployed is quite poor and not usable. Customers usually have the tendency to write feedback both on social media and or company websites if they are not happy with anything. Hence, all these feedbacks must be consolidated as customer support tickets that make their way as feedback to the respective teams involved in developing a service.

- **Feature velocity**: Feature velocity refers to the count of epics or features that are delivered by a given team, within a specified period. It is expected that during the initial periods of the project, the velocity will be low. But as the team progresses and has a strong DevOps culture, the velocity should ideally increase and reach an optimum threshold level reflecting higher productivity. The investments that are made in the initial 2-5 sprints around automation and other foundational elements usually manifest as greater feature velocity in the long term.

> **Note**
>
> Enterprises are encouraged to review the various list of metrics and select the ones that best suit their needs and purpose. The better your ability to measure is, the higher your chances are of being successful in achieving the business goals.

In the next section, we will explore a model that can be used for assessing our current DevOps maturity and identify focus areas for improvement.

Identifying the maturity index for your enterprise

All enterprises must do a self-assessment to ascertain their current maturity levels. This is required to establish a current benchmark and then set the course for future improvements.

In this chapter, we have presented a simplified *maturity model* using three levels, namely **Minimum**, **Foundational**, and **Advanced**:

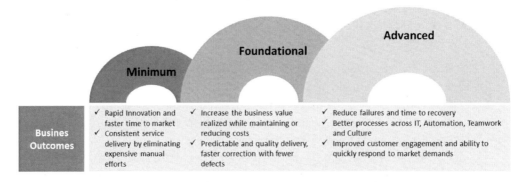

Figure 7.2 – Simple model to define the DevOps maturity level

The list of important practices or initiatives must be ranked using the maturity levels. For each higher level, the overall count of practices followed is inclusive of the practices of the lower levels. The Maturity model provides a good way to plan out your DevOps investments and initiatives.

The levels are indicative of the business outcomes that are possible for the enterprise. The higher the level, the better the alignment and outcomes on different objectives.

Let's assume that each capability area has about 10 practices. We prepare a ranking scale to define the importance of each practice by the maturity level. Certain practices are a must-have for the minimum level, whereas others are important for the higher levels.

Thus, we can create a simple DevOps maturity model as follows:

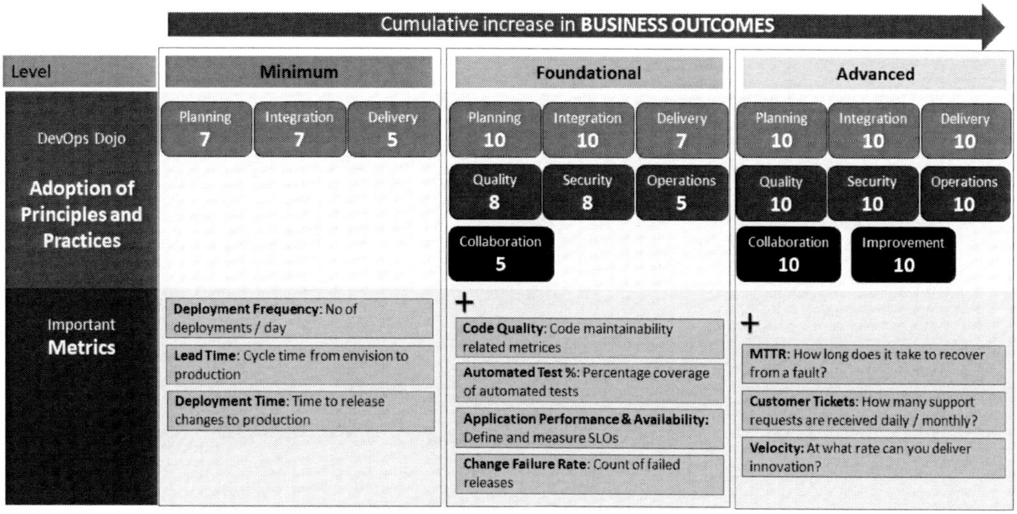

Figure 7.3 – Representative enterprise DevOps maturity model

In *Figure 7.3*, we have indicated as an example the count of practices that will be relevant at each level. Using a maturity index model, enterprises can do an internal assessment to validate their existing level, and then plan out an action to shift the needle toward the advanced level. It is evident that the business benefits increase with the adoption of greater practices within the enterprise.

Exercise

For your organization context, can you prepare a simple maturity model? Identify the important metrics that you would like to measure. Identify the challenges that you may experience while measuring them.

In the next section, we will briefly review the tools available from Microsoft to streamline and transform your DevOps life cycle processes.

The power of GitHub and Azure DevOps

GitHub and **Azure DevOps** are two powerful offerings from Microsoft that will serve as a complete DevOps toolset. From managing your backlog and team processes to a **Git**-based code repository to having the ability to execute CI/CD processes with automated testing, you will discover that GitHub and Azure DevOps are the perfect solutions for you.

At the time of writing this book, many additional new capabilities have already been planned as part of the GitHub offering and you should review the product capability page for the latest information: `https://azure.microsoft.com/en-in/products/github/`.

Read more about the Azure DevOps offering here: `https://azure.microsoft.com/en-in/solutions/devops`.

In the next section, we will cover the implementation-specific recommended guidance around some of the key DevOps practices.

DevOps in practice

Getting your DevOps strategy and implementation right depends largely on how well you can think through the importance and value-added of each practice, and convince the senior leaders and other stakeholders to share the same point of view. Without having stakeholder buy-in, some of the initiatives may not get the desired and required attention. As DevOps is a combination of people, processes, and technology, it is the people aspect that offers the most challenge when it comes to enterprise change management.

The goal of this section is to provide some ideas, tips, and recommended guidance around some of the key practices that are relevant for API-centric solutions. We shall make use of the Packt Insurance Inc. case study as a reference for the examples shared.

> **Note**
> In this section, the focus is to provide implementation-related guidance without going deeper into explaining the fundamental concepts. You are advised to review the additional reading materials to get a much deeper understanding of the areas that may be of interest to you.

Capability – continuous planning

The core objective of continuous planning is to ensure that all work that happens must be aligned with business goals. Furthermore, planning is more of an iterative process, wherein the work for the various teams (tracked as backlog/bugs/issues) must be prioritized constantly based on feedback received from users or demands of the business. This will make sure that the team can deliver incremental value with each release.

Let's review the guidance around the key practices.

Work planning using epics, features, and a user story

The first step in any software development project is to identify the functional and technical requirements that should be part of your Product Backlog. However, this backlog will not be static, but constantly evolve over the course of time and be kept updated by the Product Owner.

The product backlog is organized using epics and features. It is important that this is always based on the high-level business goals and objectives that have been envisaged by the leadership team. A simple model that represents how to organize your Product Backlog is provided here:

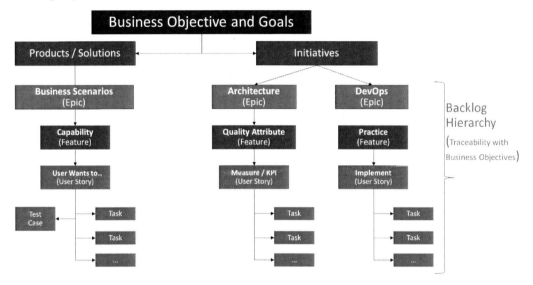

Figure 7.4 – Work planning using epics, features, and a user story

User stories typically refer to the atomic unit of work that must be fully completed to accomplish the specific user want. User stories are generally written using the **I.N.V.E.S.T (Independent, Negotiable, Valuable, Estimable, Small, and Testable)** principles. Depending on your delivery methodology followed, the size and complexity of this must be managed by your Product Owner.

Additionally, maintaining end-to-end traceability is critical to verifying whether the features envisaged have been fully implemented or not. Furthermore, as issues are identified, they can be tracked against the respective features to understand their quality.

> **Question**
>
> How are you managing the backlog for your projects? Can you identify 2-3 improvements that will make work tracking more effective for your teams with full traceability to the business objectives?

Estimation, prioritization, and release planning

Once the initial set of backlogs has been created, the development teams will then provide a high-level estimate to indicate the level of effort involved for each of the stories. You may make use of what methods suits your team, but the main idea is to create some rough order of magnitude of work planning to determine the count of resources that will be required. The Product Owner then must prioritize the stories in the order they should be implemented and come up with a release plan. The release plan presents a roadmap view of the various capabilities and when they will be available in production. The roadmaps enable the cross-functional teams to align their business processes or other dependencies accordingly.

In the following figure, we have depicted how a plan can be created of the various capabilities that have been identified for the product:

Epic	Feature	MVP (S1–S10)	Release 1 (S11–S16)	Release 2 (S17–S22)	Release 3 (S23–S28)	S29 S30
Backlog						
Epic 1	Feature A1	10 stories				
	Feature A2	30 stories				
	Feature A3		15 stories			
	Feature A4			15 stories		
Epic 2	Feature B1	40 stories				
	Feature B2	15 stories				
	Feature B3				10 stories	
Epic 3	Feature C1	20 stories				
	Feature C2		10 stories			
	Feature C3			15 stories		
Epic 4	Feature D1			15 stories		
	Feature D2				10 stories	
	Feature D3				10 stories	

Figure 7.5 – Release planning example

As evident from the figure, release planning provides a high-level view of which features will be available when. This is particularly useful when you are following a sprint-based delivery methodology. For Kanban or other delivery methodologies, this approach can be easily extended to identify the priority in which features can be released.

Backlog refinement and iterative planning

One of the most important practices for Agile and the iterative development process is to constantly refine the backlog throughout the course of various Sprints and/or releases. As enterprises are moving toward more business outcome-based IT initiatives, it is critical for the Product Owners to focus on goals that will deliver more business value as opposed to just having a wish list. Hence, planning is more of a continuous activity to achieve the desired agility in bringing innovation to the markets.

Most cloud platform providers, including Microsoft, plan their backlog for barely a quarter of a year ahead. Apart from focusing on innovations, they also make use of channels such as user voice to prioritize their backlog. This gives them the ability to meet customer demand while balancing other priorities for the team.

Capability – continuous integration

The core objective of CI is to ensure that developers adhere to some degree of discipline while creating their work products. Development teams are often composed of diverse people with varied skills and experiences. For large enterprises, often these teams are geo-distributed. By implementing proper CI practices, the team can achieve better productivity and synchronicity in action.

Let's review the guidance around the key practices.

Code repository and version control

Source Code Management (**SCM**) refers to the practice of tracking changes happening to your code base as new features and fixes are introduced. As software projects grow, the repository of code also grows with time, and hence it becomes critical to ensure that updates are merged properly without breaking anything. SCM is typically implemented through a version control tool that assists in parallel development across multiple developers using the same code repository.

In recent times, Git has become the preferred version control system for developers. A Git **repository** (**repo**) contains all the source code files that have been added by the developers along with full version history.

You can find more information about GitHub repos here: `https://guides.github.com/introduction/git-handbook/`.

While working with Git repos, one of the important decisions to take would be to follow either a **mono-repo** (single) or **multi-repo** (multiple) strategy. While there are benefits of one over the other, proper trade-off considerations must be made for your specific enterprise scenario to decide on one way or the other.

For example, mono-repos foster better team collaboration and break down the team silos at work, effecting better reuse and consistent quality through the use of standardized CI processes across the teams. On the other hand, multi-repos offer better granularity to manage disparate teams and their separate life cycles.

While building API platforms, a simple rule of thumb that you can follow is that you always start with a single repo first (even if it caters to many features or API products), and then create additional ones only when necessary to address any trade-offs. This will help you achieve better control, thereby ensuring high-quality products. Cultural change within your teams, which is the main philosophy of mono-repos, drives success in the long term.

Branching strategy

While using Git repos, you must decide on the branching strategy to be followed by the team. The **branching strategy** serves as a guide for the code promotion model for the team. When doing parallel development across multiple teams, there are a lot of modules and features for which code must be promoted by the developer from their local branch to higher branches for the CI process to complete.

In this figure, we have depicted the code promotion model in a simplified way:

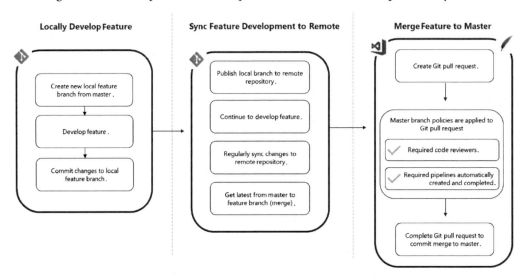

Figure 7.6 – Code promotion model for an end-to-end CI process

The most popular branching strategies are as follows:

- Gitflow
- GitHub flow
- Trunk-based development
- GitLab flow
- Oneflow

Depending on your context, you may decide to use any one of the strategies. In recent times, **trunk-based development** has gained more popularity as it focuses on bringing agility to the releases.

You can read more about trunk-based development here: `https://trunkbaseddevelopment.com/`.

Benefits of trunk-based development

Trunk-based development facilitates increased agility for development teams when releasing features to production. The feature teams will develop features using temporary and short-lived feature branches. The changes will be unit tested and verified in the development environment and then subsequently pushed to the master branch using the Git `PULL` request feature. This is explained in the subsequent sections.

PULL requests, merging, branch policies, and security

Developers are expected to merge only near-production-ready code to the master branch.

Hence, it is imperative to define a set of policies and rules that detect any violations and prevent the accumulation of technical debt that may impact the code quality.

When using Azure DevOps, adhere to the following (minimum) rules:

- Branch policy:

  a) At least one reviewer other than the developer must be mandatory.

  b) Don't allow developers to approve their own changes.

  c) Ensure you check for linked work items to maintain traceability.

d) Ensure all review comments are resolved before merging.

e) Preferably delete the feature/developer branch after merge.

f) Add additional reviewers for certain sections of code or types of files. For example, changes in any deployment-related files must also be reviewed by the DevOps lead on the project.

- `PULL` request:

  a) The developer will raise a pull request for the master branch only.

  b) Work item association is a *must* for every `PULL` request.

  c) CI build validation should pass before the code is merged into the master branch.

- Build validation:

  a) Use CI build (`GATED CHECKIN BUILD`) validation for `PULL` requests.

  b) Automatically include code reviewers – list of reviewers to be preconfigured.

- Branch security:

  a) Appropriate branch-level security should be configured so that a bypass of policies outlined is not possible.

  b) Administrative rights must be with limited team members only.

DevOps administrators can configure the rules in GitHub and Azure DevOps.

Automated CI builds

Automated CI builds will be configured using CI build pipelines (using YAML files). There may be multiple CI builds per repository. These builds will be triggered during `PULL` requests, to conduct quality checks on the developer's branch, and will succeed only if the configured rules are satisfied.

You can read more about YAML files here: `https://docs.microsoft.com/en-us/azure/devops/pipelines/yaml-schema?view=azure-devops&tabs=schema%2Cparameter-schema`.

Typical activities that will be part of the CI build process are as follows:

- Get the latest code base on the branch.
- Download any dependent packages.
- Build and compile the code.

- Check for adherence to coding standards using analyzers such as Roselyn, StyleCop, and FxCop.
- Run automated unit tests.
- Perform code coverage analysis.
- Run CredScan to detect any security vulnerabilities.
- Run an additional static code analyzer as applicable.
- When using SonarQube integration, run the sonar analysis tools.
- Check for open source vulnerabilities using tools such as WhiteSource.
- Create build output packages that can be used for CD processes.

In the next section, we have provided a checklist that you can use to verify the completeness and coverage of your unit test cases.

Checklist for automated unit tests

Developers can make use of the following checklist when writing automated unit test cases:

- Each functional requirement that applies to the class or component must have a test case of its own.
- Each design-related element that applies to the class must have its own test case.
- All unique data flows must be tested by at least one test case.
- Test cases must be defined to verify exception scenarios and invalid input states.
- Test cases must be defined for all known input-output patterns, including error scenarios.
- Test cases must be defined for all boundary conditions.

BVT automation

Build Verification Tests (BVTs) will be automated and run on every build to act as a sanity check and prevent any functional breaks as new code is being integrated.

It is recommended that BVT coverage is planned to cater to most priority 1 scenarios or happy paths of the solution. Typically, this should fall in the range of around 40-60% of the test scenarios.

For example, the following graphic depicts the sample results of a BVT test cycle run:

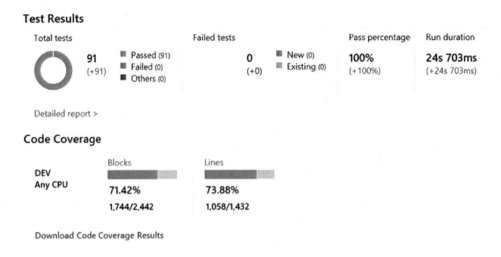

Figure 7.7 – Sample BVT automation report

BVT automation plays a very important role when any hot or urgent fixes must be deployed. The project teams will not have sufficient time to do end-to-end testing. Hence, running the BVT tests will give some degree of confidence to the project team while releasing the hotfix to production. BVT test cases must be periodically revised as new features or changes are introduced in the software.

Capability – continuous delivery

The core objective of CD is to ensure that builds are deployed to all higher environments including production as fast as possible in a fully automated fashion without incurring any major downtime that will impact the availability of the service.

Let's review the guidance around the key practices.

Infrastructure as Code (IaC)

Infrastructure as Code (**IaC**) is the management of the infrastructure and cloud services through a descriptive model as specified using templates and scripts. The templates/scripts will be versioned control within Git repos and follow the same life cycle as other code artifacts.

The primary goal of IaC is to make the provisioning of the infrastructure components immutable, seamless, and consistent across all environments by managing them through configuration. Changes that are made to definition files can be validated and then rolled out through release pipelines.

For the Azure cloud, there are various ways through which this can be accomplished:

- Azure-native SDKs
- The Azure CLI
- ARM and JSON templates
- PowerShell scripts
- Third-party/open source templates: Terraform, Ansible, and so on

IaC is a very important topic that all teams must pay attention to from the very beginning of the project. It has to be thoroughly planned and the investments in this practice will pay dividends in the long term as the systems expand and get more complex over the course of time.

Let's review the key IaC principles in the next section.

Key IaC principles

The following are the key principles that are the basis for the adoption of IaC:

- Environments can be easily reproduced.
- Environments are disposable.
- Environments are consistent.
- Environments are agile.
- Processes are repeatable.

Let's explore other important practices of CD in the subsequent sections.

Build once

The code maintained at the master branch of each repository should be near production-ready. The builds of this branch should get deployed to all higher environments as part of the release management process. This will ensure predictability and assist in the troubleshooting and reproduction of any reported incidents, in lower environments as well.

CD builds and release pipelines

The artifacts produced as output of the CD builds will be used as input while invoking automated build deployments to all environments using release pipelines in Azure DevOps.

CD builds will be configured to run automatically on completion of CI builds. These can also be triggered manually. Typical tasks that are part of CD builds are as follows:

- Create build outputs and deployment artifacts.
- Copy deployment artifacts to the build drop location.
- Create deployment packages (Docker images or Helm packages).
- Push container images to Azure Container Registry.

A **release pipeline** will typically comprise multiple **stages** (usually one per environment) and have approval gates configured as part of the standard workflow. This is to ensure that checks and balances are in place before the builds are promoted to higher environments.

In the following figure, we have depicted a sample release pipeline that depicts the flow of promoting the build from one environment to another in sequence with certain approval gates:

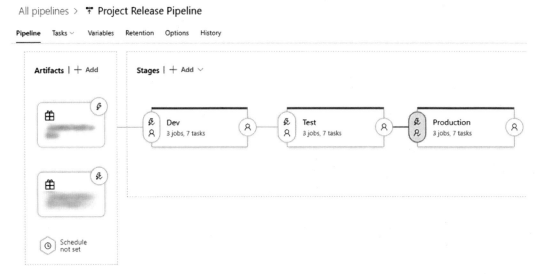

Figure 7.8 – Sample release pipeline setup in Azure DevOps

As you can observe, the build artifacts are promoted from dev to test and then to production. In the workflow, there is a gated check after each step. This ensures that environment owners have verified that the build is of good quality before approving the deployment to its respective next stage.

> **Note**
>
> The configuration of release pipelines is dependent on your repo and branching strategy. Hence, for your projects, you may have one or many release pipelines. With a good amount of modularity, better isolation and control can be obtained for various workloads or features.

Test early

Left-shift testing practices must be followed as part of the build processes to detect issues early. The objective is to mitigate quality issues early in the life cycle without waiting for them to surface through production incidents.

This practice is often undervalued by most development teams. Hence, with the demand for greater agility for the releases, left-shift testing strategies are increasingly becoming important and proper planning must be done in conjunction with other testing practices to realize the true potential of this practice.

Feature flags

Feature flagging is a programming technique that allows developers to turn a feature of a software application or a unit of business functionality on or off without having to release or changing the code in production. Wrapping code with feature flags allows developers to decouple feature rollout from code deployment. A feature flag is also called a feature toggle. However, feature flags require careful planning as the toggle shouldn't impact the normal use of the software.

The granularity of feature flags can be defined as follows:

- At a feature level (recommended)

- At a business microservice level

- At a physical service level

- At an operation level

> **Tip: Define feature flags using requirements**
>
> Feature flag requirements must be captured as part of the user stories. The impact of turning off a feature must be thoroughly analyzed before these flags are used in code. Hence, there should be a very good understanding among project teams, the Product Owner, and the solution architects on the topic of feature flags.

Canary/blue-green deployments

The feature teams will focus on building capability within the release management processes, to roll out software releases for early testing or minimize the overall downtime required for the releases.

In the following figure, we have depicted at a high level the difference between canary and blue-green deployment strategies:

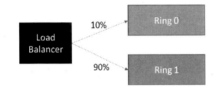
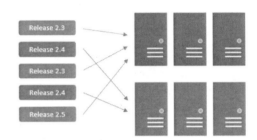

Figure 7.9 – Canary versus blue-green deployments

The specifics of the strategy will be discussed and agreed upon with the key stakeholders by defining the goals and tracking implementation through the backlog items.

For an API platform that uses AKS, you can refer to the various deployment strategies here: `https://azure.microsoft.com/en-us/overview/kubernetes-deployment-strategy/`.

Capability – continuous operations

The core objective of continuous operations is to establish practices that allow for the detection and remediation of issues after a service has been deployed and operational for end users. This is the most important capability area for running the show on cloud platforms.

Let's review the guidance around the key practices.

Security and compliance

Security and compliance-related requirements must be baked into development processes such as static code analysis and security scanning of components. Any functional or compliance-related capabilities, such as traceability and auditability, required by the platform will be captured as explicit business requirements. These requirements demand thorough analysis with respect to other requirements such as data privacy and retention before the solution is implemented consistently across the product.

Azure as a cloud platform adheres to the global standards on compliance. You can read more about it here: `https://azure.microsoft.com/en-in/overview/trusted-cloud/compliance/`.

> **Exercise**
> Review the security policy standards for your enterprise and understand how you would go about achieving them in your solution.

Continuity and resilience

Business continuity and disaster recovery processes and strategies will be clearly documented and captured. Dry runs must be conducted using non-production environments to ensure the correctness and relevance of the procedures.

Telemetry and monitoring

Both operational and business telemetry will be implemented within the platform components, to assist in the monitoring and reporting of issues.

Azure Monitor provides rich dashboarding capabilities to monitor application-specific metrics, resource health, and utilization to detect anomalies and provide timely intervention.

Some key features of Azure Monitor that you must plan to use are as follows:

- **Application Insights** for end-to-end transaction traceability, exceptions, and performance metrics
- **Container insights** for microservice usage and health-related statistics
- **Custom dashboards** tailored for use cases to track usage and reliability metrics
- **Alerts** to detect anomalies and notify the team for appropriate action

Refer to this link to know more about Azure Monitor: `https://azure.microsoft.com/en-us/services/monitor/`.

Another important resource for consideration is Azure Advisor. **Azure Advisor** periodically scans your deployed resources and analyzes their configuration and usage telemetry against best practices and rules. It then produces a report of findings categorized based on impact, along with recommendations that can help you improve the cost-effectiveness, performance, high availability, and security of your Azure resources.

In the following screenshot, we have shown a sample Azure Advisor dashboard view:

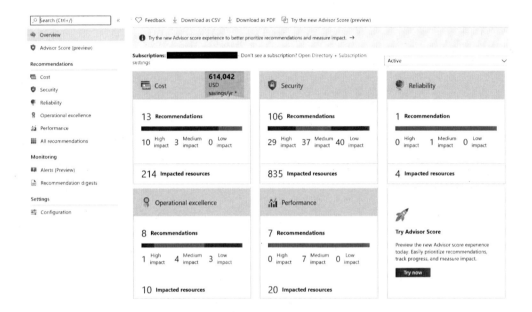

Figure 7.10 – Sample recommendations report of Azure Advisor

As part of your IT compliance strategies, ensure that these guidance and alerts are periodically reviewed by the different teams and action is taken to resolve the issues reported.

Zero-downtime deployments

Risks associated with doing deployments to production must be proactively planned and managed. Methods and techniques should be developed to minimize the impact. For mission-critical applications, any downtime on the environment will impact the business. Hence, safe deployment strategies must be implemented, such as the following:

- Deployment rings
- Blue-green deployment
- Canary deployments

> **Note**
>
> The trade-off of cost versus availability must be determined properly to be clear on the ROI. Design for zero-downtime deployments usually adds more complexity to the solution.

Shift-right testing

Shif-right testing practices offer the ability to test *preview releases* directly in the production environment. The objective is to make use of the logs and insights to verify the completeness of the feature by doing actual usage testing. This allows feature teams to reduce the cycle time through progressive experimentation using feature flags. The feature, if found faulty, can be turned off without impacting the other parts of the application.

Capability – continuous quality

The core objective of continuous quality is to ensure that checks and balances are in place to continuously evaluate the overall solution quality as new enhancements and fixes are released by the development teams. This includes both cloud foundation services and custom solution components.

Let's review the guidance around the key practices.

Quality requirements

Solution quality of service requirements (that is, non-functional requirements) will be prioritized and tracked alongside the functional backlog and implemented as part of the sprint cycles.

The **Definition of Done (DOD)** for these types of backlog items will capture the specific and measurable abilities of the solution.

Quality-driven solution design

Software design best practices will be followed for each of the components to ensure the following:

- Modularity
- Testability
- Maintainability

These practices will be defined as part of the development standards and used as a reference when doing code reviews and other discussions.

Robust unit and integration tests must be designed and implemented, which can be used during the CI build process to detect any breaks.

TDD, left-shift testing, and test automation

Test-driven development (**TDD**) practices must be used wherever applicable to improve the overall quality of the component design.

Testing processes must be automated to the maximum extent possible, covering various types of testing, so that the builds can be tested quickly in lower environments for quality certification before being moved to high environments, including production.

> **Note**
> Feature teams must prioritize automated testing strategy very early during the development cycle to benefit in the long term.

Most of the testing activities must be automated. This will expedite any testing cycles as the results can be produced within a few hours only. Furthermore, the team must constantly invest time to increase the test automation coverage.

Process and governance

The feature teams will define a list of criteria that will act as the common understanding for the DOD across various stakeholders of the project. These criteria will be used to verify the completeness of the output at the end of each sprint/life cycle stage for any backlog item.

Compliance and standards

Applicable compliance requirements for cloud resources must be codified using Azure Blueprints and deployment at the subscription and resource group levels.

Read more on Azure Blueprints here: `https://azure.microsoft.com/en-in/services/blueprints/`.

Quality measurements

The feature teams must report against the various quality metrics using dashboards. These metrics will cover all aspects that are relevant for the team to measure and monitor. Typical reports will include code quality benchmarks using SonarQube and other tools such as Velocity Charts and Defect Density.

Capability – continuous security

The core objective of continuous security is to detect and prevent security breaches from happening, as well as taking proactive measures to avoid any security incidents.

Enterprises are wary of the fact that cybersecurity threats may disrupt their business, resulting in a loss of credibility in the market. Hence, security practices must be failproof without any room for errors. Otherwise, the consequences can be disastrous. All enterprises invest in establishing a security center to monitor security threats to their IT infrastructure. Hence, running smooth cloud operations is largely dependent on how well organized your security-related practices are.

Let's review the guidance around the key practices.

Mindset and skills

Security cannot be an afterthought and must be incorporated from the very inception. The project teams must be periodically trained on various security best practices.

The teams must review the **DevSecOps guidelines** and associated toolset to implement the same for their cloud projects.

Find out more on the DevSecOps practices for Azure here: `https://azure.microsoft.com/en-in/solutions/devsecops/`.

Application and data security

Application-specific security controls will be analyzed using the security frame as described in *Chapter 3, Architecture Principles and Styles*. The identified controls must be implemented.

Data classification and associated security requirements must also be tracked as backlog items and implemented as per the design.

Periodic reviews should be conducted to revise the implementation.

Security architecture

Security must be baked into infrastructure by incorporating the guidelines from the Microsoft Cyber Security Reference Architecture. You can read more on that here: `https://www.microsoft.com/security/blog/2018/06/06/cybersecurity-reference-architecture-security-for-a-hybrid-enterprise/`.

You must track all the requirements using the backlog so that the compliance status can be tracked.

Security controls will be designed and baked into the scripts for infrastructure provisioning.

Identity and access management

For Azure cloud environments, identity and access management must be controlled using Azure AD and RBAC permissions. Proper user management policies must be deployed to prevent any unauthorized access.

Secure operations

Azure Security Center, Azure Monitor alerts, Azure Sentinel, and other related toolsets must be used to offer secure and reliable operations.

Capability – continuous collaboration

The core objective of continuous collaboration is to achieve greater productivity by eliminating silos and improving communication and collaboration across different team members. High-performance teams are ones where the members demonstrate greater coordination to achieve the common goals for the team. That comes with autonomy and empowerment.

Let's review the guidance around the key practices.

Alignment and autonomy

Each of the feature teams must be self-sufficient in terms of skills required to deliver the stories. Autonomy is fundamental to ensure the smooth running of day-to-day tasks and operations. However, there is also a need for tighter alignment on the overall goals across the various feature teams.

Various feature teams must conduct joint planning sessions to identify all dependencies and establish clear expectations of each other during the planning. A better alignment will lead to a good outcome. Otherwise, chaos may prevail while the teams try to do their best within their known boundaries and constraints.

Kanban collaboration

The feature teams should make use of Kanban boards to track work progress. The boards will comprise stages and allow the ability to visualize the status of various user stories, tasks, or bugs as they progress through the stages.

Wiki and teams collaboration

It is recommended to maintain all documentation as wiki content. Various team members can then easily collaborate on the wiki content for their respective areas. Wiki content is authored using **Markdown (MD)** files.

You can read more about it here: `https://guides.github.com/features/mastering-markdown/`.

Documentation often becomes stale if not maintained periodically. Hence, by managing it in a wiki alongside your code, you can implement and follow the life cycle processes consistently. Whenever any major design decisions are taken or code or a deployment artifact is modified, the associated documentation must be updated as well.

Broadly, you can think of structuring your wiki content as follows:

- Solution overview
- Architecture and design
- Work tracking and team processes
- Developer guide
- Environments and deployment guide

Thus, we can see that by adhering to the best practices of doing reviews, maintaining MD files alongside code, and so on, the whole process of creating documentation gets simplified.

Capability – continuous improvement

The core objective of continuous improvement is to facilitate the identification of improvement areas either by channeling the feedback received or by detecting deviation from the established metrics. Enterprises may have a certain degree of DevOps maturity, but they must take all feedback to improve upon their existing processes and methodologies.

Let's review the guidance around the key practices.

Measuring success through metrics

You must identify the important DevOps-related metrics that apply to your business/enterprise context. Valuable actionable feedback is obtained only when there is a clear way to measure the efficacy of your DevOps practices. Furthermore, this serves as input to garner support from the leadership team to move the big rocks that may pose challenges.

We discussed some of the DevOps metrics earlier in the *DevOps metrics and their importance* section in this chapter. All teams must identify the critical metrics and then track them throughout the life cycle stages.

Continuous feedback

Feedback must be sought from all important stakeholders periodically by using surveys to identify what is working and what needs improvement. Agile is all about change. So, teams must establish a culture of improvement, by acting on the feedback received. This is very important as the priorities may change over a period of time, requiring better adaption or even other practices that may add value.

Value stream mapping

It is recommended that the teams conduct a **value stream mapping** exercise to determine both the business workflow and process improvements that can bring greater efficiency within the enterprise.

You can read more on value stream mapping at `https://en.wikipedia.org/wiki/Value-stream_mapping`.

The important point to note would be that software products developed are largely dependent on the existing business processes. Hence, modeling and creating a map can yield improvement ideas, with a focus on identifying opportunities for optimizations.

Pillar – culture

For the team to succeed in the various DevOps initiatives, there must be a strong cultural alignment and inclination toward progressive ideas. Most of the DevOps initiatives will fail if there is no team buy-in. There is a typical tendency to stick to what has worked in the past. However, for all enterprises, modernization of their DevOps practices for accelerated cloud adoption is the only way forward.

You can read more on the cultural mindset attributes here: `https://docs.microsoft.com/en-us/learn/modules/introduce-foundation-pillars-devops/3-explore-first-foundation`.

Pillar – lean product

It is encouraged that teams follow a product-centric model while building any software solutions. This is very important while building enterprise solutions such as API platforms.

A product-centric model offers greater agility in bringing innovation to the market. The Product Owner (who owns the backlog) focuses on building features prioritized as part of the digital strategy and what can bring revenue or value for the enterprise.

Products add to the brand value and evolve over a period. You can read more about the product-centric model: `https://docs.microsoft.com/en-us/learn/modules/introduce-foundation-pillars-devops/4-explore-second-foundation`.

Pillar – architecture

In *Chapter 3*, *Architecture Principles and Styles*, and *Chapter 4*, *Assuring the Quality of the API Service (or Product)*, we discussed how the architecture of a solution is dependent on the non-functional requirements or qualities that must be met. Hence, the team must create backlog items for all such requirements. Some of them get addressed in the design, and the remainder has to be handled through the implemented solution.

You can read more on the architecture pillar here: `https://docs.microsoft.com/en-us/learn/modules/define-foundation-pillars/2-explore-third-foundation-pillar`.

Pillar – technology

One of the crucial enablers for DevOps is the list of tools and technologies used by the team to implement the various processes and practices. GitHub and Azure DevOps bring an amazing experience for the development community. The toolset is robust and caters to most requirements. Additionally, Azure provides a wide range of other services to derive insights around topics such as security, monitoring, and deployments.

Hence, teams must be thorough with their usage of the various tools to maximize the benefit derived from their DevOps practices.

You can read more about the technology pillar here: `https://docs.microsoft.com/en-us/learn/modules/define-foundation-pillars/3-explore-last-foundation`.

In the next section, we will review a sample approach of how project teams can track important DevOps-related initiatives as a project backlog.

Tracking DevOps initiatives in the backlog

All initiatives and activities performed as part of DevOps must be tracked using the backlog. This is the only way that effort can be prioritized within the stipulated timeframe to accomplish the desired goals.

As an example, we have demonstrated how easily you can capture these initiatives in the form of a backlog under an epic within Azure DevOps:

Order	Work Item Type	ID	Title	State
1	Epic	1168	> 👑 Architecture	● New
2	Epic	2617	⌄ 👑 DevOps	● New
	Feature	2618	> 🏆 Continuous Integration	● New
	Feature	2621	> 🏆 Continuous Delivery	● New
	Feature	2627	⌄ 🏆 Continuous Operations	● New
	User Story	2755	> 📖 As a DevOps Engineer, I want to verify if the monitorin...	● DOD Ready
	User Story	17503	> 📖 As an operations analyst, I want to create metrices fro...	● DOD Ready
	Feature	2628	🏆 Other Practices	● New
	Feature	2629	> 🏆 Continuous Quality	● New
	Feature	2630	> 🏆 Continuous Security	● New

Figure 7.11 – Tracking DevOps activities as a backlog in Azure DevOps

Tracking everything as a backlog will offer the ability to prioritize tasks for the available capacity. *If it's not in the backlog, it will never get done.*

Summary

In this chapter, you understood the importance of having the right set of DevOps practices. DevOps is a combination of people, processes, and technology. So, enterprises must establish the right mindset and orientation to go about implementing the practices with due diligence. It's crucial to have a vision and foresight as the results will be seen in the long term. There has been sufficient research already conducted in this space and there is guidance available for teams to absorb, learn, and march forward in the right direction.

All developers must transform themselves into DevOps engineers, to equip themselves with the concepts and practices that are necessary to master to build solutions for the cloud.

In the next chapter, we shall look at some of the tools that are useful for designing, building, and testing API-led architectures.

Further reading

- DevOps Dojo White Belt foundation documentation: `https://docs.microsoft.com/en-us/learn/paths/devops-dojo-white-belt-foundation/`

- O'Reilly book on DevOpsSec: `https://www.oreilly.com/library/view/devopssec/9781491971413/`

- Data-driven DevOps metrics by Gartner: `https://www.gartner.com/en/documents/3760663/data-driven-devops-use-metrics-to-guide-your-journey`

- *Accelerate: The Science of Lean Software and Devops: Building and Scaling High Performing Technology Organizations*: `https://www.holistics.io/blog/accelerate-measure-software-development`

- Scaled Agile framework for Lean enterprises: `https://www.scaledagileframework.com/`

- Git branching strategies for your team: `https://gitential.com/git-branching-strategies-for-your-team-how-to-choose-the-best/`

- Git branching guidance: `https://github.com/MicrosoftDocs/azure-devops-docs/blob/master/docs/repos/git/git-branching-guidance.md`

- Canary deployment strategy for Kubernetes: `https://docs.microsoft.com/en-us/azure/devops/pipelines/ecosystems/kubernetes/canary-demo?view=azure-devops&tabs=yaml`

- Value stream mapping reference: `https://tallyfy.com/value-stream-mapping`

- Introduction of DevOps Dojo: `https://devblogs.microsoft.com/devops/intro-of-devops-dojo/`

Section 3: Deliver Business Value for a Modern Enterprise

This last section will help you understand how IT strategies must be aligned with the core vision of the company, as set forth by the executive team, to thrive as a digital business in this ever-growing competitive landscape.

This section includes the following chapters:

- *Chapter 8, API-Centric Enterprise Integrations*
- *Chapter 9, API as a Monetized Product*

8
API-Centric Enterprise Integrations

Enterprises and their technology uses have been evolving constantly since the launch of cloud technologies. This has resulted in the need to develop integration interfaces to support **interoperability** across various systems and applications. The adoption of API-led architectures is vital to the success of these **Enterprise Application Integration** (**EAI**) scenarios. API solutions can revolve around business entities or domain models, thereby enabling standardization across all the integrating parties.

The purpose of this chapter is to take a deeper look into some real-world enterprise integration scenarios and explore how the **Azure Integration Services** offering can be utilized to build modern API-based integration platforms. Most of the popular players in the **Enterprise Resource Planning** (**ERP**) space, such as Microsoft Dynamics, SAP, Oracle, and TIBCO, are adopting industry-standard protocols and patterns for their interfaces as well. Hence, enterprise solution architectures are increasingly shifting toward standardization, as the maintenance and upgrading of standardized interfaces is simpler than for custom-built solutions.

In this chapter, we are going to cover the following main topics:

- Exploring EAI

- The rise of **Integration Platform as a Service (iPaaS)**

- Implementing EAI patterns using iPaaS

- API management

- Understanding the Azure Integration Services offering

By the end of this chapter, you will be able to design EAI workflows in Azure. You will also develop a good understanding of the importance of API-centric solutions for various enterprise integration patterns. Moreover, you will learn how to make use of Azure services such as API Management, Logic Apps, Service Bus, and Event Grid to make the right implementation choices for your iPaaS platform requirements on the Azure cloud.

> **Enterprise integration patterns**
>
> Enterprise integration patterns are established patterns or messaging flows that are used to exchange information across two different software systems within an enterprise. These systems can be either internal or external to an enterprise. You can read more about enterprise integration patterns here: `https://www.enterpriseintegrationpatterns.com/`.

Exploring EAI

EAI typically involves a variety of products and technologies, making EAI complex to achieve. Also, besides the technical challenges, the complexity of the organizational structure and any associated IT management strategies brings further challenges to the situation. The main causes of failure to achieve EAI are the constraints of cost and insufficient tooling support to orchestrate the integration workflows. Most legacy applications have limited support for integration models.

However, over time, certain patterns and standards have been established to streamline integrations. The adoption of API-led architectures has allowed application developers to open up legacy applications that were otherwise difficult to integrate with. The domain of EAI has gained popularity among enterprise architects, as they have found solutions to tackle integration and interoperability challenges across different types of applications.

Key initiatives toward a digital enterprise

The COVID-19 pandemic brought conventional businesses almost to a standstill. Enterprises that had an online presence were able to still stay in business and stay connected with their customer base. Traditional enterprises took the brunt of dwindling sales and losses. Hence, it has become abundantly clear that enterprises have to focus on key businesses drivers such as improving their business agility, introducing multiple channels of distribution, creating differentiated services, and offering the ability for customers to connect using devices of their choosing.

So, for an enterprise to become a truly digital enterprise, they must prioritize the following initiatives to transform themselves:

- Converge on the ability to connect key apps to enterprise data.
- Build lightweight mobile apps that connect with business logic backend APIs.
- Establish processes that allow devices to communicate with the cloud and vice versa (using the **Internet of Things**, or **IoT**).
- Offer self-service API subscription management through a developer portal.
- Ensure the end-to-end security of data during transit and storage.
- Use flexible delivery models to meet specific business needs.

In the next section, you will find strategies to open up a legacy application using an API-centric solution approach.

Modernizing legacy applications using APIs

The term **legacy application** refers to systems that are old and can easily be replaced by newer products or technologies. However, it may not be straightforward to change them if they see enterprise-wide usage. As more modern applications are developed and more API-led strategies are adopted, it is becoming imperative to allow interoperability with legacy applications.

The following are a few ways in which legacy applications can continue to be used alongside modern applications:

- Develop a **wrapper API** (REST or RPC) to internally connect to legacy systems. That way, all new applications can follow the modern way of API-led connectivity.

- For systems that act as master data stores for an enterprise, develop a layer of **data services** (accessible over HTTP). These services can be consumed by applications that require access to the master data catalogs.

- **Refactor** and **rehost** the code of the legacy system as a microservice that is exposed through an API. This type of migration is expensive but offers more flexibility and performance, which is ideal if the legacy system is business-critical in nature.

In the next section, we will review some common API use cases by industry.

API use cases in the enterprise

Based on the size of the enterprise and product offerings, there may between a dozen and hundreds of public and private APIs. With the adoption of microservices architectures, these numbers can easily go higher. The greater the granularity, the better the management life cycles of these APIs.

While API requirements vary by industry, API platforms are generally indispensable as they make information exchange seamless. Let's review some of the common use cases across various industries:

- **Retail**: Retailers use APIs for inventory management, sales, invoicing, packing and shipping products, managing customers and online stores, and even collecting customer feedback.

- **Supply chain**: Most manufacturers need to allow integrations with their internal ERP systems. Furthermore, they must decouple their business data from the applications that generate it.

- **Financial**: APIs can be used to manage everything from customer accounts and ledgers to online bill payments and transfers. Financial systems require highly secure and reliable API systems. They require omnichannel access to customers' financial data.

- **Healthcare**: APIs can offer access to patient information data to other providers or insurance companies for more automated bill processing. Healthcare has many uses for API platforms when it comes to providing efficient and effective patient care.

- **Transportation**: APIs are used for geo-mapping to provide real-time updates en route, data on the availability of transport vehicles, predicted times of arrival, and other analytics.

- **Government**: APIs are used for authorized access to public records, the raising of complaints, citizen utility services, and tax records. APIs can help citizens to interact with the government and receive information in a timely manner.

You have seen that APIs have widespread application across various industries. In the next section, we will discuss the benefits of iPaaS platforms hosted on the cloud and why enterprises can use them for all integration requirements.

The rise of iPaaS

Cloud adoption is on the rise, and most modern enterprises have started investing in building a cloud-based iPaaS solution for connectivity across applications, systems, and platforms on the cloud and on-premises. This allows building loosely coupled integration flows without needing to deploy any middleware applications. Let's take a closer look at what an iPaaS platform is.

What is an iPaaS platform?

To put it in simple terms, an **Integration Platform as a Service** or **iPaaS** platform is a suite of services deployed on the cloud to enable the onboarding and execution of integration flows that connect various internal and external systems hosted on the cloud, or even on on-premises networks, using industry-standard protocols.

The basic features of an iPaaS platform include the following:

- Provide communication protocol connectors (for HTTP, SFTP, AS2, AMQP, and more).

- Support application connectors, including SaaS and on-premises applications.

- Handle data formats such as JSON or XML and data standards such as EDIFACT and HL7.

- Orchestration and routing of messages.

- Data validation and transformation.

- Monitoring and insights.

- Full API life cycle management.

- Tools for the development and deployment of services.

Initially, you may start with simple integrations and slowly expand on your integrations portfolio to include complex and mission-critical flows.

Types of integrations

iPaaS platforms allow seamless data exchange within the organization and without, while ensuring security and data privacy controls. iPaaS platforms have great potential and must be made a part of the core business strategy. They act as a bridge between the consumer or partner applications and internal systems while offering a hassle-free integration experience. As the integrations are developed using industry-standard protocols and patterns, their reach can easily be maximized.

There are three classifications of integrations:

- Application-to-application (that is, EAI), or **Point-to-Point (P2P)**
- **Enterprise Service Bus (ESB)**
- **Business-to-Business (B2B)/Electronic Data Interchange (EDI)**

Depending on the type of industry and the IT maturity of the enterprise, one or more of these patterns will be used.

Benefits of iPaaS

Over the past few years, there has been a gradual shift toward the adoption of SaaS-based solutions in most large enterprises for various business process workflows. The key driving factor has been the ease of use and standardization available, which is lacking in custom line-of-business applications.

Additionally, there has been demand for a hybrid cloud setup, wherein the business has the flexibility to onboard newer workloads on the cloud while still managing legacy applications on-premises with seamless and highly secure integration between the two, using virtual networks, ExpressRoute, or site-to-site VPN topologies.

This created an opportunity for cloud-based integration channels as enterprises did more business with their partners and vendors. As an outcome, iPaaS platforms started gaining popularity as such solutions can be quickly deployed using cloud-native capabilities, thereby reducing the time needed to onboard integration workloads.

The primary benefits of an iPaaS platform for an enterprise can be broadly classified into external and internal benefits. Each category is explained briefly in the following sections.

External benefits

External benefits refer to the experience of the consumers (customers, vendors, or business partners) who integrate their existing apps with the enterprise or consume their digital services using published interfaces. Businesses are investing in technology and increasing their digital footprint. Hence, consumers can benefit immensely from iPaaS platform offerings in several ways.

The external benefits offered by iPaaS platforms can be broadly summarized as in the following sub-sections.

Integrated single solution

iPaaS platforms generally encapsulate all the underlying complexity behind any specific integration flow. Hence, consumers needn't worry about the technologies used by the enterprise or their associated complexities. All they have access to is a centralized platform solution that is made of standardized protocols and schemas. This makes the experience of all consumers consistent and uniform, making it quite convenient for them to connect to and reap the benefits of the platform.

Central repository of data

For consumers, iPaaS platforms act as the entry-point of access to a central repository of data. This is because all data services are exposed using the iPaaS platform. Hence, the discovery of and access to any enterprise dataset is organized in an easy-to-interpret manner. This makes it quite useful for all consumers.

Transparent information exchange

As consumers have access to a shared data repository, all members receive the same information when requested. Hence, there is total transparency in information exchange, thereby preventing any misinterpretation. Also, once submitted, data is persisted in the shared data store.

Improved business workflow

The use of multiple tools and technologies often introduces additional complexity that impacts business workflows. The users of the system are forced to make use of multiple tools to get a task done. This results in delays impacting productivity. An iPaaS solution eliminates this problem as it offers a more efficient environment for business process flows. Also, automated monitoring and alerting will improve the overall operations life cycle.

Internal benefits

Within an enterprise, iPaaS platforms are also utilized internally by various business units for information exchange to facilitate business processes. The benefits derived by the business through the internal usage of iPaaS platforms are known as **internal benefits**. The usage of a common set of tools within an enterprise increases the overall efficiency of business workflows.

The primary internal benefits of using an iPaaS platform are as follows.

Avoidance of departmental silos

Large enterprises, without centralized IT management, invariably end up with different tools for their integration requirements. This results in the formation of departmental silos as data resides in disparate systems. This formation of islands of data stores is detrimental to the organization as there is no easy way to derive end-to-end business insights from the data saved in these systems.

Robust and centralized iPaaS platforms can eliminate these silos. Teams are forced to use the same standards for integration and data exchange, thereby reducing the need to build duplicate systems for the same data. This makes the data easily accessible to all stakeholders within the organization to visualize insights according to needs.

Near real-time processing

By adopting efficient message processing strategies, iPaaS platforms can handle API requests faster, thereby providing almost instantaneous access to processed data. This removes any delays due to manual processes, and business rules can be easily automated to handle the data that gets submitted to the platform.

Increased rhythm of business

iPaaS platforms prevent data loss, thereby ensuring that all information stored in the systems is accurate and up to date. This helps in achieving an increased rhythm of business as all decisions are based on true facts as presented by the underlying data.

Centralized management

As explained earlier, iPaaS platforms act as a single window for the discovery and usage of data services. This improves the overall management of IT systems as the data is managed centrally, thereby adhering to IT best practices.

Reduced or optimized operations cost

Managing a wide spectrum of software systems adds to the overall operations cost of maintaining them. iPaaS platforms reduce the need to create duplicate systems that do the same thing. The cloud resources used by these platforms can be shared, and hence their usage will be more optimal due to multitenancy.

In large enterprises, IT can own the iPaaS infrastructure and then cross-charge business units using a pay-per-use model. This will offer a cost advantage to the business units, as for them, the ROI can be utilized almost instantly.

Improved security and compliance

Security and compliance go hand in hand whenever it comes to managing data. Consistent implementation of the policies and guidelines is always a challenge. Different stakeholders have different understandings of the rules. Hence, by having a centralized iPaaS platform, compliance requirements can be better managed.

Security threats are ever-increasing, and specialized skills are required to secure a platform. iPaaS solutions offer an advantage here as the ownership of security lies with a single team that owns the platform. It is certain that compliance will be consistently applied across the shared iPaaS platform.

In the next section, we will look at a typical iPaaS architecture for the Azure cloud.

iPaaS architecture for the Azure cloud

Azure offers a wide variety of services that can be used to build an iPaaS platform. A high-level conceptual view of the iPaaS architecture in Azure follows:

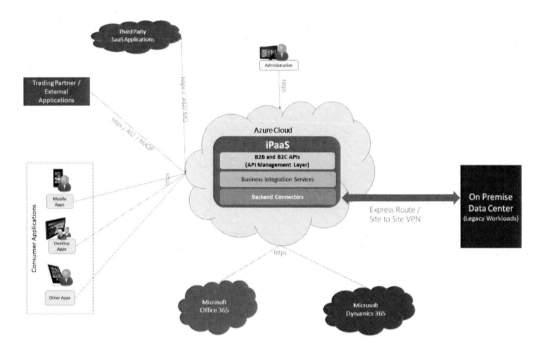

Figure 8.1 – Conceptual view of the iPaaS architecture of Azure

The basic foundational blocks of the iPaaS platform comprise the following:

- An API management layer hosting the B2B and B2C public APIs. These APIs can support a variety of protocols according to industry standards.

- A business integration services layer containing the core business logic for data input validations, rules execution, and transformation to canonical form.

- Backend connectors that allow data to be routed to the respective target destination. These systems can be different, hence the connectors offer the ability to route the data to multiple destinations as per any requirements.

An iPaaS platform acts as the centralized integration layer for an enterprise and offers connectivity across a wide variety of consumer applications, external or third-party services, and even other Microsoft clouds such as Office 365 or Dynamics 365. Even legacy workloads residing on on-premises data centers can be easily connected and accessed.

A simplified view of a typical iPaaS pipeline is as follows:

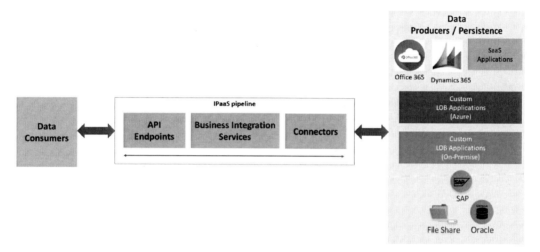

Figure 8.2 – Typical iPaaS pipeline for an enterprise

You have seen that data consumers (both external and internal) can access data produced by a variety of applications using centralized data processing and access pipelines hosted by an iPaaS platform.

In the next section, we will study the implementation of iPaaS alongside EAI patterns.

Implementing EAI patterns using iPaaS

EAI solutions typically target the following primary application integration patterns:

> The goal of this pattern is to replicate the data changes that occur in one application to other applications that must be notified about the changes. This will ensure that all systems are updated with the latest information. For example, when a customer updates their information in, say, a CRM system, the changes are updated in billing systems or other systems that make use of customer data:

- **Data consistency integration:**

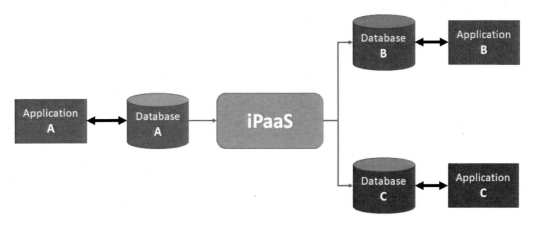

Figure 8.3 – Data consistency integration pattern

This is the most common integration pattern among all EAI flows. An end-to-end business workflow execution may involve multiple systems or applications that are mutually independent, each having its own specific function. These applications will take part in the various steps of the business workflow, wherein the outputs from one system can serve as input to the other systems.

Typically, these systems belong to specific departments or organization units, and they execute the respective sub-processes with the information available. For example, in a manufacturing scenario, when a purchase order is received, it may trigger workflows for the Packaging department and the Billing and Invoicing departments to create the invoice. Once a payment is received for the purchase order, the Packaging department is told to ship the order:

- **Business process-based integration:**

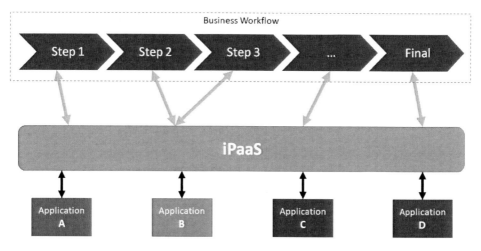

Figure 8.4 – Process-based integration pattern

This type of integration is used in scenarios where the target application comprises multiple sub-systems. The **initiator** (**source**) of the data flow is notified of the success of the operation only when all the underlying composite blocks of the target application are completed successfully. These types of flows require careful planning as data must be maintained in a consistent and correct state across the various applications that are involved in the flow. Composite applications can fully encapsulate a business process or be a step in a multi-step process flow:

- **Composite application integration:**

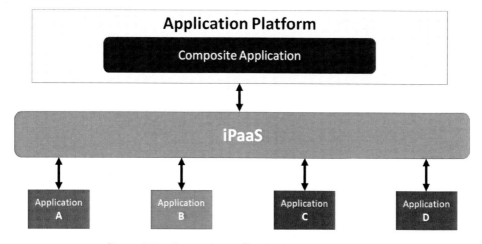

Figure 8.5 – Composite application integration pattern

In the next section, we will review the API management solution capabilities that any iPaaS platform must have.

API management

iPaaS platforms are never complete without an API management solution. The **API management** layer offers discovery and access to the list of published APIs that have been activated for the integration flows.

There are five main capabilities of an API management solution. They are as follows:

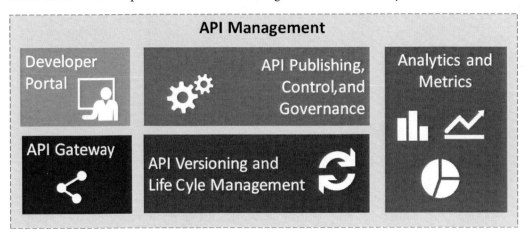

Figure 8.6 – API management solution capabilities

These capabilities are briefly described in the following sections.

API gateways

An **API gateway** acts as the entry point for all your APIs. It provides the infrastructure necessary to host and manage the high availability of the public endpoints.

An API gateway regulates the way that consumers access the published APIs, with or without authentication. It protects the data accessible through the API services by preventing any unauthorized access. These gateways make the consumption of the APIs easy and simple. As an outcome, enterprises achieve reduced integration time and enhanced customer experience through the quick onboarding of developers, partners, and subscribers for the API.

API publishing, control, and governance

API management solutions must support the **publishing** of APIs. Basically, this means that APIs can be easily added to an API catalog and published for use by external and internal consumers. APIs can be added by uploading a standard specification file, such as OpenAPI Specification, or using an administrative interface.

The API management features like rate limiting (traffic throttling) and load balancing helps avoid disruptions to your API processes. The incoming requests are throttled by rate limiting; it limits the number of API requests made to a said API in a given time frame.

Load balancing, on the other hand, helps you leverage a number of gateways for a single API; this distributes the incoming requests across the various gateways. Both these features target good response times and reduce the overall error rates or failures of the APIs.

An API management solution also provides secured and controlled access to your APIs. For example, developers or consumers will be issued access or **subscription keys** that must be passed using request headers or query string parameters while invoking the APIs. In the absence of these keys, users will be denied access to API operations.

Developer portal

The API **developer portal** is primarily targeted at the developer community, who will build applications that consume the list of published APIs. A robust and resourceful developer portal provides developers with the necessary resources to rapidly create cloud applications or services with their APIs. Typically, these include the following:

- API catalog
- Documentation about the API operations and their usage
- Wiki pages or other content
- Assets such as videos, quick starts, and development kits

Developers can quickly go through all the information and understand how to make use of the APIs in their projects. A developer portal can help drive innovation and increase the re-use of your APIs. By extending the capabilities of the developer portal, enterprises can achieve self-service-based paid distribution channels, thereby increasing the revenue generated through the iPaaS platform.

API versioning and life cycle management

Managing the life cycles of APIs is equally as important as the other features we've been talking about, especially because new enhancements or features are constantly being rolled out. Hence, an API management solution provides all the tools and infrastructure needed for planning, designing, implementing, testing, publishing, operating, consuming, maintaining, versioning, and retiring your APIs.

A **life cycle management** function enables the version control of APIs, ensuring backward compatibility to avoid disruption to any existing processes and allowing developers access to the latest versions of services to implement them in their applications. API life cycle management offers the ability to boost your digital innovations by ensuring consistency across all the API development teams within an enterprise.

Analytics and metrics

An API management solution provides useful analytics based on the monitoring and telemetry data captured by the tool. This is important to understand and analyze the various **Key Performance Indicators** (**KPIs**) or metrics for the API landscape.

Various dashboards and charts can be prepared using this metrics data to detect issues or security threats, measure performance, and analyze exceptions and availability challenges. Furthermore, reporting on usage trends, user segmentation, the geo-distribution of consumers, and more offers business insights into the target user base to help the enterprise plan for marketing activities. API insights play a vital role in the overall API strategy for an enterprise.

Azure API Management

Azure API Management (PaaS) offers a robust API management solution for your iPaaS solutions on the Azure cloud. We will briefly discuss the capabilities of Azure API Management in subsequent sections. However, you can read more about it here: `https://azure.microsoft.com/en-in/ services/api-management/`.

In the next section, we will review the Azure Integration Services offering, which comprises a set of Azure services that can be used to build your integration flows.

Understanding Azure Integration Services

Microsoft provides **Azure Integration Services** for enterprises to build iPaaS solutions on the Azure cloud. The following has been said regarding Microsoft's place in Gartner's Magic Quadrant:

> *Microsoft is placed in the leader quadrant for the enterprise integration platform as a service space.*

The amount of services and their range of configuration and connector options makes Azure Integration Services a rich offering that differentiates Microsoft from other competitors in the market. Azure provides four core things to form the critical features required to accomplish enterprise integrations:

- The ability to **publish API endpoints** for discovery and use
- The ability to **create and run integration** logic business workflows (**orchestration**)
- The ability to **design and implement** loosely coupled integrations by using a **messaging** stack
- The ability to **handle communication** via **events** to trigger processing pipelines:

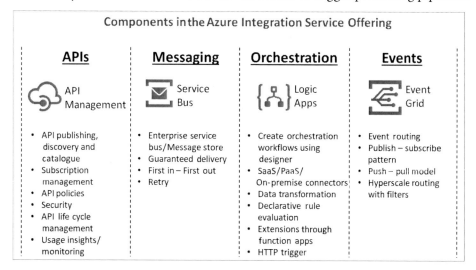

Figure 8.7 – Azure Integration Services

You can read more about Azure Integration Services here: `https://azure.microsoft.com/en-us/product-categories/integration/`.

Code-based customizations

Azure Functions is used to build extensions or code-based logic that can be invoked either directly or from Logic Apps.

Let's explore the iPaaS building blocks of Azure in more detail in the next section.

iPaaS building blocks of Azure – explained

The four main components that are used to build the iPaaS platforms in Azure are as follows.

Azure API Management

Azure API Management (**APIM**) is a managed PaaS offering that allows organizations to publish APIs to both internal and external consumers. With Azure APIM, you can publish APIs that can be hosted anywhere. Basically, it allows for the decoupling of actual API hosting from a published gateway that acts as a **single entry point** (**façade layer**) for the full landscape of APIs published by the enterprise:

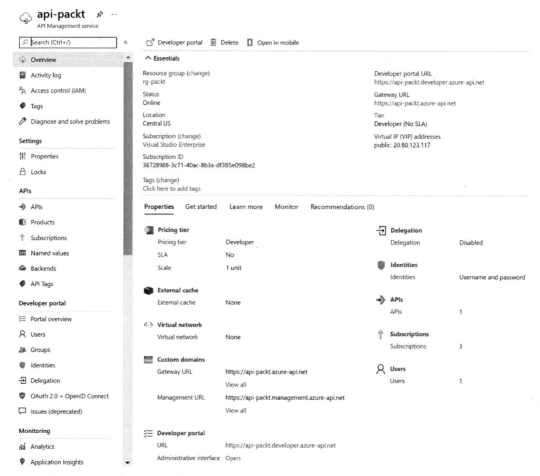

Figure 8.8 – Azure APIM – Overview

As a PaaS solution, it is basically composed of three parts:

- **API gateway**: This serves as the infrastructure hosting the load-balanced endpoints that serve the different API requests. When using a virtual network-based topology, the gateways can be deployed to multiple Azure regions, thereby improving the availability of the service. The key functions of APIM are as follows:

  a) Accept API calls and route them to the respective backend services.

  b) Verify API keys, OAuth tokens, certificates, and so on.

  c) Enforce quota usage and rate-limiting throttles.

  d) Handle advanced policy configurations such as response caching, request and response modifications, and more.

- **API publishing and configuration management (directly through the Azure portal)**: The Azure portal provides the ability to directly create and configure the API, along with other configuration options. Using the Azure portal, you can do the following:

  a) Import APIs using OpenAPI Specification files (YAML/JSON) or define the API schema directly.

  b) Create a logical grouping of APIs as products. An API can belong to one or many products.

  c) Configure and use various policies such as quotas or transformations. The policies can be applied at the product, API, and even operation level.

  d) Specify authentication and access for end users.

  e) View various built-in analytics reports. Configure additional logging as applicable.

- **API developer portal**: This serves as the main portal for developers who will consume the APIs. The API developer portal can be used as a branded website. The main features are as follows:

  a) Display the API documentation and allow developers to try out the API operation to check whether it's working.

  b) Manage user subscriptions and keys.

  c) Review API usage and other metrics.

  d) View generic content as published by the administrators.

> **Note**
>
> You can read more about Azure APIM here: `https://docs.microsoft.com/en-us/azure/api-management/`.
>
> Also, here is a reference architecture for Azure APIM for a very basic enterprise integration: `https://docs.microsoft.com/en-us/azure/architecture/reference-architectures/enterprise-integration/basic-enterprise-integration`.

Logic Apps

Azure Logic Apps is another useful PaaS offering that brings in the power of orchestration and automation for your no-code workflows. Each logic app implements a workflow that represents a business process or just a pure integration scenario. Logic Apps can be used to connect two different systems or even two different applications.

A logic app comprises a **trigger** and series of steps that can be either **loops, conditional statements**, or **actions**. A sample representative view of the designer is shown here:

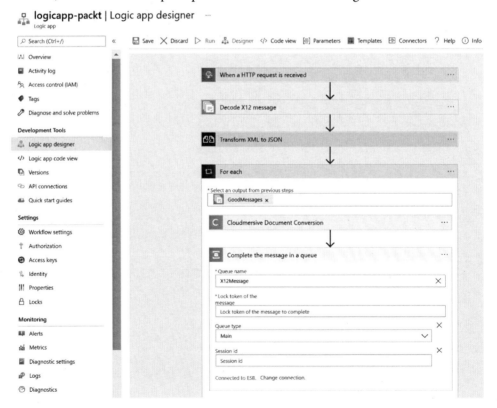

Figure 8.9 – Logic app designer

The rich capabilities supported by Logic Apps include the following:

- Easily create workflows using the (web) designer.
- Support for a large number of connectors, including SaaS and on-premises connectors.
- Highly scalable and reliable; build mission-critical workflows that can run 24x7.
- Workflows can be version-controlled using ARM templates and DevOps.
- Enterprise integration capabilities are available through integration accounts.
- Automate business processes and connect on-premises, hybrid, and cloud applications.
- Leverage **Azure Machine Learning** and **Azure Cognitive Services** while building smart integrations.

Building integration workflows using logic apps is really fast and enterprises can benefit hugely from using the large number of connectors that are available.

Service Bus

Azure Service Bus is used in application integration scenarios where asynchronous communication techniques are preferred. Communication happens using messages:

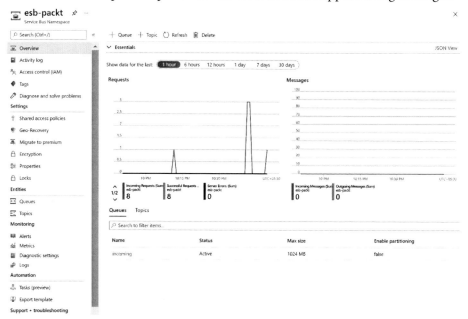

Figure 8.10 – Azure Service Bus Overview page

The salient features supported by Azure Service Bus are as follows:

- High availability and disaster recovery, including geo-replication of the namespaces
- Queue semantics and ordered delivery of messages, that is, **First-In-First-Out (FIFO)**
- Supports rich filters while reading messages
- **Push-Pull (queue)** or **Publish-Subscribe (topic)** models

For enterprise messaging scenarios, you can choose between **queues** and **topics** depending on the nature of the integration pattern.

A **queue** is like a FIFO message delivery mechanism from a sender to a receiver. Basically, the sender will deliver messages to a queue, which will then be received by a single consumer to subsequently process the message. There may be multiple consumers of a queue, but each message will be delivered to one consumer only:

Figure 8.11 – Queue with multiple messages

These are the key features:

- Ordered message delivery through sessions
- Stores the message until read by the receiver
- Preferably used in point-to-point messaging scenarios, wherein the sender writes the message to the queue, and after the receiver has read the message, it is deleted from the queue

Topics and **subscriptions** are used in scenarios where the same message must be delivered to multiple receivers simultaneously in a one-to-many form of communication. Here, the receivers *subscribe* to a particular topic. As the messages are received for a specific topic, it is forwarded to all subscriptions registered with the topic:

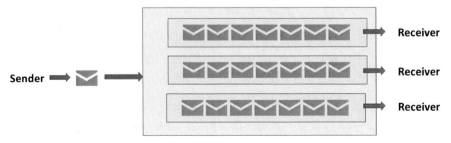

Figure 8.12 – Topic with multiple subscriptions and messages

Here are the key features:

- Supports delivery of the same message to multiple subscribers.

- Used in publish-subscribe scenarios, wherein the sender writes the message to the topic, and the topic delivers the message to the subscribers.

- Multiple independent subscriptions are possible, based on message property filters or rules.

Read more on when to use what here: `https://www.serverless360.com/blog/azure-service-bus-queues-vs-topics`.

Event Grid

Azure **Event Grid** is another PaaS offering that enables integration scenarios involving messages. It operates on the event publisher/event subscriber pattern. Basically, **event publishers** are systems that send notifications regarding any changes happening in them. These notifications or messages are then routed to the **event subscribers**, which receive the message and then execute additional actions based on the update received.

You can read more about the concepts of Azure Event Grid here: `https://docs.microsoft.com/en-us/azure/event-grid/concepts`.

A brief overview is depicted here:

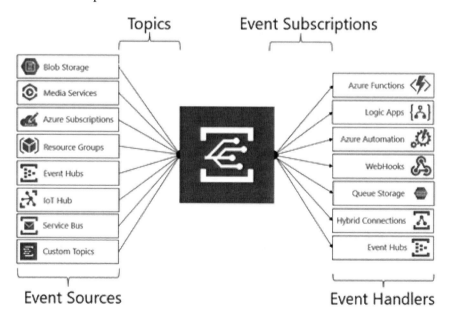

Figure 8.13 – Azure Event Grid overview

The key concepts you need to remember are as follows:

- **Events**: What happened
- **Event sources**: Where the event had originated
- **Topics**: Where the publishers will send the events
- **Event subscriptions**: Registrations based on the type of events to receive
- **Event handlers**: The app or service that receives the event and handles it

In the next section, we will study how to make use of the various components of Azure Integration Services to develop integration flows.

Using Azure Integration Services

Azure Integration Services has many applications within an enterprise, especially in building EAIs. Some of the common scenarios include the following:

- Interconnecting various enterprise apps within an organization (using EAI flows)
- B2B/trading partner integrations (using EDI flows)
- Integrating line-of-business applications with SaaS products/services
- Event publishing scenarios/IoT-based integrations

The following are a few examples of reference architectures.

Extensible EDI flows

Electronic Data Interchange (EDI) is a commonly used integration pattern in manufacturing, wherein trading partners send orders, invoices, credit notes, and so on for reconciliation with the enterprise's back office, warehouse, or ERP systems:

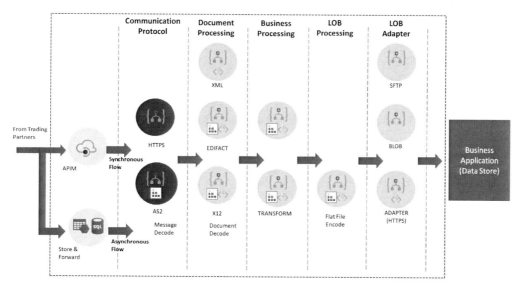

Figure 8.14 – Extensible EDI flow integration

You can read more about EDI integrations here: `https://docs.microsoft.com/en-us/azure/logic-apps/logic-apps-enterprise-integration-x12`.

Command message

The **command message** pattern is generally used to invoke workflows or state changes in a system by sending a command after the occurrence of a business event or state change in another system. It is the simplest type of message-based integration:

Figure 8.15 – The command message integration pattern

Message routing/event messaging

Event messaging or **message routing** patterns are used in scenarios wherein a large stream of messages is sent by event producers and must be routed to appropriate destinations depending on some filter criteria. The event sources write to a common endpoint, and then the Event Grid system routes to the respective subscribers listening to the topics. The event handlers, configured per subscription, route the event messages to the appropriate destination applications:

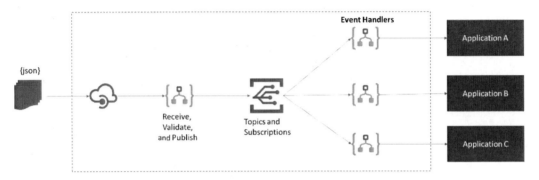

Figure 8.16 – Event messaging integration pattern

The patterns and scenarios listed here are only a limited subset to demonstrate how easily you can build integration flows in Azure. For a more detailed study, please go through the references provided at the end of this chapter.

Summary

In this chapter, you have learned about the role and importance of API-centric architectures for enterprise integration scenarios. You have also studied how enterprises can benefit from implementing iPaaS platforms on Azure that will enable them to modernize their EAI flows and connect the legacy workloads with a larger ecosystem of applications, including SaaS and cloud-native applications.

By now, you must be familiar with using Azure APIM as the single entry point for all your API-based integration workflows. You should also be able to design and implement mission-critical and highly reliable integrations using various Azure resources such as Logic Apps, Service Bus, and Event Grid. The flows can be implemented as data processing pipelines.

In the next chapter, we will extend the concepts presented so far and explore strategies to monetize your API solutions.

Further reading

- Enterprise integration patterns using Azure Integration Services: `https://platform.deloitte.com.au/articles/enterprise-integration-patterns-on-azure-intro`

- Reference on enterprise integration patterns on Azure: `https://platform.deloitte.com.au/articles/enterprise-integration-patterns-on-azure-platform`

- Architect API integration in Azure: `https://docs.microsoft.com/en-us/learn/paths/architect-api-integration/`

- Azure Integration Services: `https://azure.microsoft.com/en-us/product-categories/integration/`

- iPaaS benefits: `https://blog.dreamfactory.com/ipaas-benefits-8-reasons-why-businesses-are-flocking-to-integration-platform-as-a-service/`

- *The Ultimate Guide to iPaaS*: `https://blog.hubspot.com/marketing/ipaas-guide`

- Send and receive X12 messages: `https://docs.microsoft.com/en-us/azure/logic-apps/logic-apps-enterprise-integration-x12`

9
APIs as a Monetized Product

By definition, a **product** is a service or an item that can be in cyber form as well. It can be sold at a price in the market that is competitive and appropriate, depending on the nature of the item. For an enterprise, APIs are the medium by which innovation is brought to the marketplace. They want to capitalize on the opportunity by introducing new products and services and by establishing new ideas, differentiating the business from the competition.

Businesses rely heavily on digital distribution channels to market and sell their products and generate revenue. APIs foster a growth outlook as businesses can expand beyond their standard operating models. Building and managing API platforms has been recognized as a core enterprise strategy. The APIs provide access to the business assets of an enterprise. Hence, this API economy targets revenue generation through direct or indirect use of the API ecosystem that provides or processes business data.

Organizations have already started exploiting the commercial benefits of an API strategy. They can easily sell these channels of interaction using an intelligent pricing model.

The purpose of this chapter is to provide an overview of the concept of *the API as a monetized product*. Organizations are heavily investing in API-led digital assets as they are consumable by any channel or platform.

In this chapter, we are going to cover the following main topics:

- APIs as digital assets

- Exploring business drivers of monetization

- API monetization models

- API production in Azure

- API consumption – rate limits and quotas

- Measuring API consumption

By the end of this chapter, you will understand how to envision API products, how to devise consumption models, and apply a monetization strategy to generate revenue from the API investments.

APIs as digital assets

The potential for APIs to be seen as digital assets is huge. Organizations are constantly evolving business strategies to tap into this opportunity for their revenue generation. When envisaged with a long-term strategic outlook, productized APIs can offer a significant advantage over other distribution channels. Effective monetization strategies with a variety of consumption models can lead to upselling and cross-selling opportunities for the enterprise.

By actively monitoring the value derived from their API investments and the associated business analytics, organizations can establish different business models to suit the needs of the customer. Self-service, subscription-based engagements are becoming quite popular these days, especially in the media and consumer service industries.

Growth of the API economy

Since the inception of **Service Oriented Architecture (SOA)**, there has been a gradual shift toward decoupling frontend applications from the business layer, which are getting exposed as APIs. As a matter of fact, *APIs are everywhere today,* all-pervasive in the digital experiences that any of us are engaged in.

The API economy has created a demand in the marketplace for enterprises to expose business data and services through APIs, with the eventual goal of generating revenue through them. APIs simplify access to the data and information in a secured manner. Application developers can easily integrate with the APIs and build user-focused apps. App developers can pay attention to building the experience without really worrying about how the API has been implemented.

The adoption of cloud-based technologies has generated a need for enterprises to modernize their legacy applications at a rapid pace. The erstwhile **monolith** applications are now redesigned or refactored using microservice API-driven architectures. The rapid expansion in the usage of **mobile computing** and **IoT** has made it imperative for enterprises to adapt to the market demands and build APIs that allow devices to seamlessly connect and exchange information.

The API value chain

So far, you have learned that APIs play a vital role in the digital transformation strategy of any business. The growth of the API economy has led to a complete paradigm shift in the way enterprises do business with their partners and customers. The broader objective is to use the power of data to generate business value within the ecosystem. Let's discuss the key players in this API value chain in the following section.

Participants in the API value chain

The key participants in the API value chain are depicted in the following diagram:

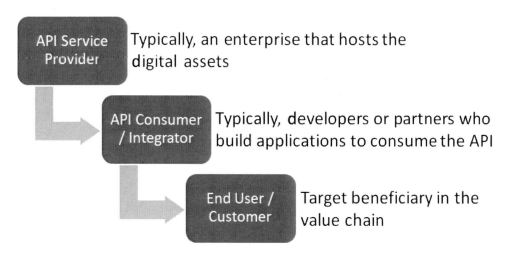

Figure 9.1 – Participants in the API value chain

Let's discuss the main participants and the roles they play in the value chain:

- **API Service Provider**: This refers to the organization that exposes APIs to facilitate the use of the business capabilities or provide end user digital services. They define the pricing plans and usage guidance for the APIs. They provide governance over the API platform and manage the reliability of the service as per the agreed SLAs.

- **API Consumers** or **Integrators**: This refers to the developers or partners who consume the APIs directly or build end user applications that integrate with the APIs. The consumers must follow the rules of engagement while consuming the APIs. They may require prior registration with the API provider before being allowed access to the APIs.

- **End Users** or **Customers**: This refers to the users of the applications who receive the benefits of using the API. The users may not be directly aware of how the APIs are invoked or used, but their usage of the various capabilities drives the overall consumption of the APIs.

For true value realization of the APIs, all three participants in the value chain must benefit in one way or another. For the enterprise, having the right monetization strategy is fundamental to driving consumption and usage. Consumption drives revenue, leading to the creation of a digital asset.

In the next section, we will review the business drivers of API monetization.

Exploring business drivers of monetization

Enterprises must adopt a mindset of innovation to survive in the market. Hence, they must be responsive to the demands of the business and create products that showcase their unique brand and expertise. There are several reasons for an enterprise to expose business functionality or render a digital service through an API that can be monetized. The main business drivers for this approach are explained in the following sections.

Expand the channels of revenue streams

By monetizing APIs, enterprises can create a new opportunity to generate revenue. APIs can deliver a virtual service or business functionality for a price. The consumers of the APIs will be charged based on their consumption of these APIs, and the revenue collected through the use of the APIs will add to the revenue stream of the enterprise.

Some companies have totally transformed their businesses and sell API products like **Software-as-a-Service** (**SaaS**) products. There is a billion-dollar market for this. Examples include Azure Cognitive Services, Twilio, PayPal, and Salesforce. Most of these companies adopt an API-first strategy while implementing their solutions so that it is easier for them to introduce API products into the market.

Capture analytics for improved marketing strategies

Studying user behavior provides useful insights into the segmentation and preferences indicative of the market they are in. Since data is the new currency for innovation, many companies have developed APIs that collect data and gain insights into customer behavior when they use any application.

Companies such as Microsoft and Google offer products that have API interfaces, which application developers can consume and integrate while building their own applications. The insights derived from the ingested data are extremely valuable and crucial to deriving marketing strategies. This user-generated data can be further augmented using machine learning and artificial intelligence capabilities to make predictions on the adoption and use of the applications.

Companies can easily go out of business if they don't pay attention to improving the quality of their services based on the critical factors that emerge from the data.

Enhance brand value through customer loyalty

The brand image of a company is enhanced only when customers stay loyal and use their products. Customers share their first-hand experience of using the service, which has a huge influence on other potential buyers. Hence, by creating APIs that can be easily consumed and used for various business workflows, enterprises can generate some loyalty toward their platform.

If the companies do not offer public APIs that can be consumed for integration with their various solution capabilities, customers can easily switch to competitors who might have a better offering available in the market.

For example, **SAP Ariba** is a SaaS product that allows APIs for enterprise integration purposes. **Line of business** (**LOB**) applications can easily integrate with SAP Ariba using REST APIs. This has conferred a competitive advantage on SAP, which was previously primarily an on-premises solution.

Foster innovation through new product capabilities

APIs serve as backend services for any web, mobile, or even desktop application. Enterprises may expose APIs to allow application developers to integrate with their backend data. This decoupling of UI and backend paves the way for new capabilities to be offered by the applications that would not have been possible otherwise.

For example, by consuming the Microsoft Cognitive Services Vision API, application developers can easily build applications that analyze image data to extract meaningful information by processing the captured image. Image recognition has a variety of use cases, starting from, say, face recognition pattern matching to authorize door entry, to storytelling for paintings in an art gallery, to creating in-store experience in retail outlets. The possibilities are endless.

Stay relevant in the marketplace

Most organizations are transforming themselves through digital investment to stay relevant in the market. As the technology landscape is evolving, the industry is moving at a rapid pace to bring in new ways of connecting with its customers. Organizations are adapting to the demands of the market to stay in the competition. API-based platforms provide the most effective way to achieve agility and diversify the modes of interaction.

For example, most multiplex theatres allow third-party apps to be integrated with their APIs. This allows the user to book a ticket from an app of their choice. While the theatres may charge a nominal fee for such integration, the app owners can also sell other items through the same channels.

Thus, for an enterprise, all digital initiatives must take into consideration the business drivers for better alignment and sustainable growth in the long term. In the next section, we will review the various monetization models that can be used for your API economy needs.

API monetization models

There are various options when it comes to monetizing your APIs. Enterprises may choose one or more options, depending on their business strategy.

The most widely used monetization options are depicted in the following image:

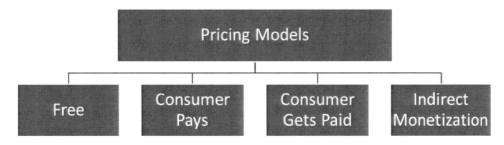

Figure 9.2 – API monetization models

Let's review each option in more detail.

Free

One of the most common ways to get developers to start using your APIs is to offer a **free tier**. There are zero charges to be paid by the consumers while using your APIs. This model is suitable when the API made available is a low-value asset or a shared service, and you can rely on other mechanisms to generate revenue.

For example, application developers can integrate with identity providers such as Microsoft, Facebook, or Google to implement OAuth-based authentication within their apps for free. While these APIs are free to use, the providers can attract many users to register with their platform. This gives them access to a community of consumers to whom they can reach out to sell other products through their platforms.

Sometimes, enterprises also put a capacity limit on these free APIs. This helps them prevent degradation of the performance of the APIs if many hits are made to the API. This is particularly advantageous for developers when they are building solutions in the beta stage.

Careful consideration must be taken before making APIs free to use. As businesses run on profit, alternate revenue streams must be available to compensate for the operational expenditure on these APIs.

Consumer pays

In this model, the consumer of an API is required to **pay** as per the rate plan published by the API service provider. The enterprises levy a charge that is appropriate to recover the capital and operational expenditure of building and managing the API business asset.

There are additional sub-models for charging the API consumer:

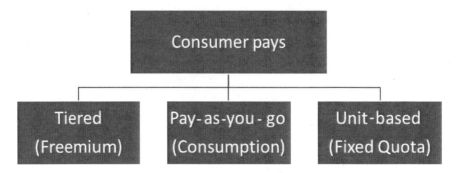

Figure 9.3 – Pricing options for charging the consumers of an API

- **Tiered**: In this model, the API publishers may define tiers in which the rate charged to the consumer will vary. For example, there may be no charges up to a certain limited usage, but when the limit is breached, the consumers will be charged. Further, the tiers can be such that consumers can get a discount based on their usage volume.

  Most API providers typically implement this model. They use a variety of naming conventions to define the multiple tiers, such as Basic, Standard, and Advanced, or even Gold, Silver, and Bronze. The developer subscribes to the pricing tier that's suitable for their needs. Usually, once the threshold of consumption for any given tier is reached, the service is disabled until the next payment cycle, or the service charges have been paid for by using a top-up mechanism. Optionally, the API service providers may give an option to automatically switch tiers if the consumption exceeds the tier's threshold.

  Enterprises usually get creative when coming up with pricing plans using the tiered approach. They attempt to keep the rates optimal to attract the greatest number of developers to their API platform.

- **Pay-as-you-go**: In this model, the rate charged is dependent on the actual consumption of the API consumer. This is advantageous for the consumer in comparison with other pricing models as they only need to pay for what has been used. However, this pricing strategy works for only a limited set of features. For heavy usage scenarios, this model may be quite expensive for API consumers.

  In a pay-as-you-go pricing plan, a base rate is defined, which is used to calculate the charges. For example, let's say that every API request will be charged at *$0.01*. So, if the API consumer makes *1,234* requests overall, then the charge for consumption will be *1234 x $0.01 = $12.34*.

For API service providers, offering this model may be risky due to its unpredictable nature. If the load pattern on the API infrastructure varies all the time, there may be performance issues. This model requires careful planning on the service provider side before being included as one of the pricing options for the API.

- **Unit-based**: In this model, the price is fixed based on a unit-based rate over a certain period (such as daily, weekly, or monthly). The API service providers arrive at this rate by taking into consideration the expenditure that will be incurred for the infrastructure components hosting the API, and some profit over the cost.

  For example, let's say that the API requests will be charged at *$0.50* per *1,000* requests daily. This constitutes 1 unit, and the consumers can purchase one or many units depending on their predicted consumption.

  Once the request count reaches the upper limit of units purchased, no further API calls will be allowed. The consumer will need to purchase additional units to continue using the service. Hence, this model is also known as *fixed quota*.

  This model offers uniform and predictable revenue generation for the service providers. However, developers or consumers suffer a small loss if the count of API requests is less than the quota allocated.

The consumer pays model requires careful evaluation to arrive at the appropriate pricing strategy. It is often used as an upgrade to a free offering to attract customers to a premium membership.

Consumer gets paid

In this model, the consumer of the API receives a monetary incentive for integrating with the API. This drives the adoption of the API in the marketplace and encourages more consumption and usage.

Here are the sub-models within this model:

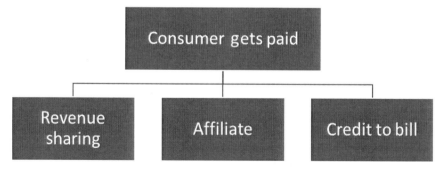

Figure 9.4 – Options for the consumer gets paid model

Let's discuss each of them in detail:

- **Revenue sharing**: In this model, the API consumer is paid a commission for using the API. The consumer acts like a broker, or an agent, thereby assisting in increasing the consumption of the API.

  The API consumers provide the ability within their app to invoke these APIs as the user browses through the application.

  A typical example is the Google AdSense API. The consumer apps capture the user behavior with their tool and send all of this information to the AdSense API.

- **Affiliate**: In this model, the consumer advertises the service provider's capabilities in their apps or websites. Users visiting the consumer apps may be interested in the offerings from the provider. Any sales that happen after that are treated as revenue earned through a reference, and a portion is paid as commission to the consumer.

- **Credit to bill**: In this model, the provider will give back credits, earned through revenue sharing or affiliate models, to the consumer on their bill as discounts. This will reduce the cost for the developer directly as the bill will be lower. This model is typically followed by a small group of service providers who interact and integrate through their apps.

As is evident from the options mentioned here, this strategy is a win-win situation for both the consumers and the API service providers. Hence, this can be seen as a more lucrative model for the consumers.

Indirect monetization

Indirect monetization is another common scenario, where the revenue is earned through indirect means without requiring the consumer of the API to explicitly pay for their API consumption. Most enterprises build and expose APIs to accomplish specific business goals. These APIs are integrated within LOB applications or even third-party applications. These applications generate revenue for the enterprise through the various business scenarios, resulting in indirect revenue creation through the use of the exposed APIs.

Some common sub-models within this model are as follows:

Figure 9.5 – Indirect monetization models

Let's explain these sub-models in detail:

- **Brand awareness**: Sometimes, companies make certain APIs available for free to use in any third-party application. These APIs typically strive to create awareness of its services and products to end users. This way, brand awareness through directed marketing campaigns can be achieved.

- **Content acquisition**: Companies may also provide APIs that may be used to add or publish content or datasets. Through this mechanism, enterprises can acquire content for their business use that can be further extended by deriving business insights.

- **SaaS offering**: Many software vendors typically also publish an API layer for all their business applications. By adopting this strategy, they can easily resell their API services through an SaaS model to businesses or individual users. This creates more opportunities as the consumers don't have to purchase the packaged applications.

- **Internal consumption**: APIs can also be developed for internal consumption within an enterprise. Business units may build customer-facing applications by using the APIs. This leads to revenue generation through customer engagement. The business units might have a charge-back model to recover the cost of managing the APIs. Additionally, the internal use of the APIs help to improve productivity, reduce errors, and reduce development costs.

- **B2B partnership**: In a **business-to-business (B2B)** partnership model, APIs are used to achieve seamless business integration of the various workflows. This has been studied in some detail in the previous chapter. By opening their backend systems through APIs, enterprises achieve more agility, thereby leading to better coordination and enhanced partnership for mutual growth and benefit.

In this section, you reviewed the various monetization strategies that can be used for your API solutions. You must carefully plan and choose the model that may apply to your specific business context. In the next section, we will explore how this monetization aspect can be put into action when implementing and deploying API solutions in Azure.

API productization in Azure

In this section, we will review the high-level approach to creating and publishing productized APIs using Azure API Management and other necessary services. An end-to-end solution requires multiple components to be developed, hence the objective here is to provide a big-picture view of how to approach your API monetization strategies from a solution standpoint.

> **Note**
>
> The following concepts are just a starting point and are not meant to be a comprehensive solution. You are encouraged to elaborate on the key points and discover additional requirements that may be required for your specific business context.

Through the next sections, you will learn how to approach your monetization plans using a good productization strategy. You will also learn what Azure services need to be considered as part of your solution.

Requirements summary

At a high level, the overall functional requirements can be categorized into three buckets, namely **Productization**, **Platform Administration**, and **Consumer Experience**:

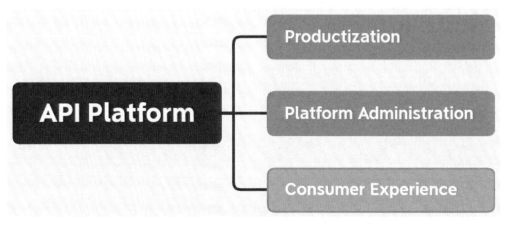

Figure 9.6 – High-level categorization of the feature areas

The capabilities within each feature area are explained in more detail in the following sections.

Productization

The primary focus of the **Productization** feature area is to identify and define the monetized APIs, along with their management and selling strategy as digital products. Hence, it covers capabilities such as identifying variants of the products and their corresponding mapping to physical assets, a definition of the pricing and rate plans (along with the necessary metadata), and content that must be created for driving the consumer experience:

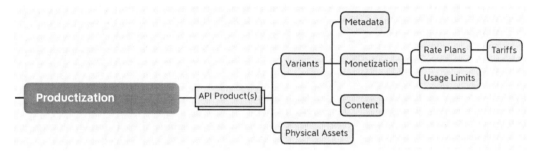

Figure 9.7 – Desired capabilities of Productization

The top-level capability blocks are briefly explained here:

- **API Products** – This refers to the catalog of APIs that will be made available to the consumers.

- **Physical Assets** – This comprises the actual cloud services that are part of the specific API product and their corresponding life cycle management. The operations cost of maintaining these services must be considered while deriving the pricing plans.

- **Variants** – This identifies the variants of any API product that will be monetized. Define and create the content (textual, PDFs, images, and so on) that is required for the marketing strategy. Define the various pricing plans to make it attractive for the consumers.

Now, let's move on to **Platform Administration**.

Platform Administration

Platform Administration focuses on the overall hosting, management, and governance of the API platform, along with the administration of the various LOB applications/services from an end-to-end solution perspective. The major focus areas here are **subscription management**, **billing and invoicing**, and generating **business insights and analytics** to present the overall health of the service from financial and operational standpoints:

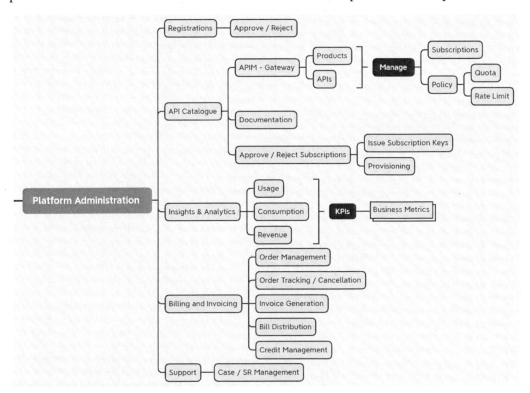

Figure 9.8 – Desired capabilities under Platform Administration

The top-level capability blocks are briefly explained here:

- **Registration** – Identify how users will register with the platform. Define any approval workflows that are necessary depending on the user segment.

- **API Catalogue** – Identify the API assets that will be published through API management. Apply policies to control access and usage of the APIs. Manage the subscriptions of the users.

- **Insights and Analytics** – Capture telemetry data to generate the various metrics. Visualize the data using different dashboards (such as Power BI) to derive the various insights that are required for business and IT decision-makers.

- **Billing and Invoicing** – Define the workflows related to subscriptions, order management, billing, and invoicing.

- **Support** – Establish tools and processes to handle support requests.

Next, let's take a look at Consumer Experience.

Consumer Experience

The adoption of the API platform is heavily dependent on the ease with which consumers can discover the APIs they need, review the specification and technical content (by browsing through the developer portal), register to subscribe and pay for their selected product, and then start using the API in their applications.

The **Consumer Experience** is largely driven by the brand management and marketing strategy of the organization. It is recommended that you start small and make use of end user feedback to improve the value provided by the solution.

Consumer experience is typically delivered through a web portal and/or a mobile app. Azure AD B2C can be used to facilitate user registration and identity management, including making use of **social OpenID** identity providers such as Microsoft and Google:

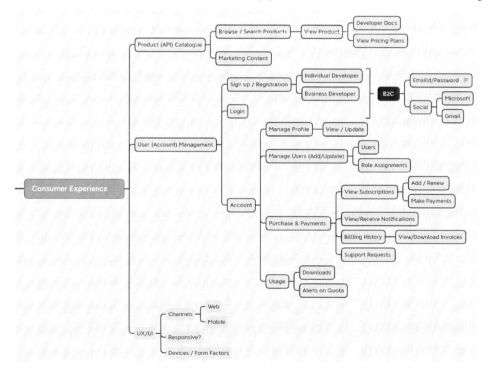

Figure 9.9 – Desired capabilities under Consumer Experience

The top-level capability blocks are briefly explained here:

- **Product (API) Catalogue** – Create the marketplace experience for the users (both anonymous and registered).

- **User (Account) Management** – Establish the procedures for registration and login based on the type of user. Include preferences to use existing social identity providers.

- **UI/UX** – Identify and define experience for the channels that will be supported for the end user experience. Include multi-device, multi-form-factor capabilities, along with modern UI design. Enrich the experience through usability studies.

The capability maps listed earlier can be further expanded to create a more detailed Product backlog. It is recommended that you analyze this and come up with your own *Epics*, *Features*, and *Stories* to define your product roadmap.

In the next section, we will study how Azure API Management and other services can be utilized to develop a solution catering to your API productization strategy.

Solution approach

As we saw in the previous chapter, **Azure API Management** (**APIM**) is a robust product offering in Azure that can be used for API governance and life cycle management strategies. Hence, the **solution approach** for API monetization relies heavily on the usage of the native capabilities available in the APIM managed service. The high-level building blocks for the proposed solution are depicted in the following diagram:

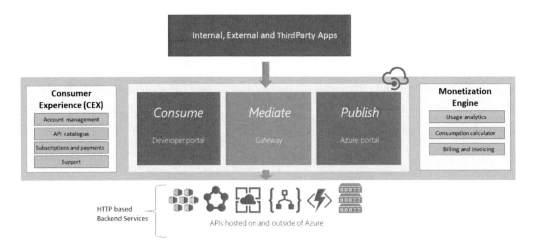

Figure 9.10 – Solution building blocks

As you can see in *Figure 9.10*, APIM is the key solution component supported by additional capabilities that will have to be developed leveraging **Commercial-off-the-shelf (COTS)**, SaaS, or even custom solutions depending on their suitability for the business context.

The high-level conceptual view of the end-to-end solution is presented as follows:

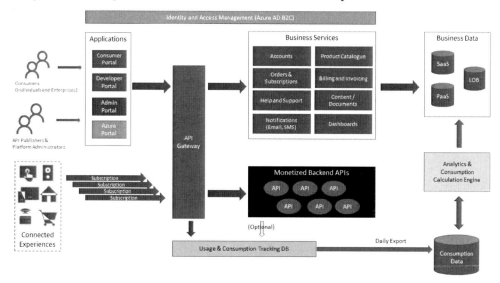

Figure 9.11 – High-level conceptual view

From the conceptual view, we can easily see that there are a few moving pieces in the overall solution. Hence, technology choices relating to these pieces must be made to achieve a cohesive experience for end users. In any enterprise context, some of these pieces must be custom-developed, while some others can be integrated using a plug-and-play model. In the next section, we will review a few of the important capabilities that will be accomplished using APIM.

API products and publishing in APIM

API publishing in APIM involves uploading the OpenAPI specification files (YAML/JSON) that define the operations and other behavior of the API.

APIM has a feature called **Products**, which is technically just a logical grouping of APIs so that a common set of access policies and rules can be applied. However, it must not be confused with the term **API Product**, which is purely a business offering created for the purpose of monetization. In the following sections, we will cover how to model your APIM products and APIs design in order to implement the monetization strategy defined for the corresponding API product.

Let's consider an example to understand this. Say there is an API product named Quoting Service that comprises three SKUs: Basic, Standard, and Premium. For simplicity purposes, we will consider that these SKUs differ by their request limit quotas and associated charges, as shown in the following table:

SKU or Pricing Plan	Plan Details
Basic	No charges, fixed quota of 100 API calls per hour
Standard	$10, fixed quota of 1,000 API calls per hour
Premium	$100, unlimited API calls per hour

So, from a monetization strategy perspective, we have just one API product (a single backend service) but three different pricing plans.

One of the ways the product and pricing plans can be implemented in APIM is as follows:

1. Create one API entry for the Quoting Service API using the OpenAPI Specification files of the backend service.

2. Create three different products within it, namely Quote Service (Basic), Quote Service (Standard), and Quote Service (Premium).

3. Map the Quoting Service API to the three different products in APIM.

4. Configure settings and policies on the products as per the pricing plan.

Your API now has the requisite configuration to support the various pricing plans.

The process is depicted in the following diagram:

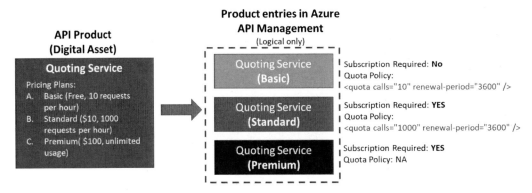

Figure 9.12 – API Product versus APIM (Logical) Product entry

You can read more about rate limits and quotas here: https://docs.microsoft.com/en-us/azure/api-management/api-management-sample-flexible-throttling#rate-limits-and-quotas.

> **Note**
>
> Depending on the nature of the API product and its monetization strategy, alternative permutations and combinations may be explored. You must consider the various factors, such as subscription management, traffic isolation, rate limits, quotas, and more, while coming up with the structure.

In APIM, the product entries would look something like this:

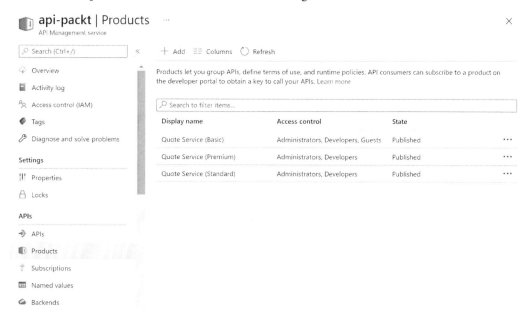

Figure 9.13 – Product entries in APIM

Observe that **Quote Service (Basic)** is accessible to **Guests**. This makes the API visible to anonymous users in the Developer portal, whereas the remainder are available only to registered developers.

Subscription management

Developers who want to consume paid APIs must create a subscription and then pay for the charges as per the pricing plan. The design of the business workflow for creating a subscription is outside the scope of this book. However, the net result of the workflow is the generation of a **subscription** key, which must be configured in APIM to activate access for the API.

You can read more about subscriptions in Azure APIM here: `https://docs.microsoft.com/en-us/azure/api-management/api-management-subscriptions`.

Subscription is the most important concept in APIM. Developers must pass the subscription key in the HTTP request while calling the API (operation) endpoint. Consumption data is recorded based on the subscription key. Hence, these keys should be securely managed to prevent any malicious access.

Subscriptions can be managed at the product level, as shown in the following screenshot:

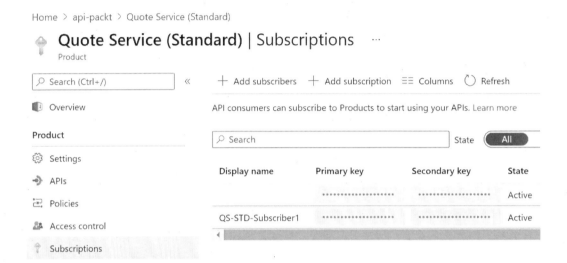

Figure 9.14 – Managing subscriptions for a product

Authorization policies

To secure access to the API, additional configurations such as OAuth 2.0 or client certificates may be implemented at the APIM layer. Hence, for the client applications to consume the API, all the necessary information must be part of the HTTP request.

API consumption – rate limits and quotas

Rate limits and quotas are used for the API monetization strategy. They define the maximum limits that apply to the subscribers of the APIs. Additionally, different subscribers can have different rate limits or quotas based on the plans they have subscribed to.

Rate limits are used to define certain thresholds to limit the count of requests, thereby preventing any unexpected spikes during the usage of the API. Rate limits are also used to enforce any monetization rules relating to the subscription limits.

Quotas are typically used to define the usage volume of an API over a long period. This is useful for creating tiers based on **usage volume targets**. Quotas are like rate limits, but they are generally used with a large window of time.

You can read more about them here: `https://docs.microsoft.com/en-us/azure/api-management/api-management-sample-flexible-throttling#rate-limits-and-quotas`.

Now, let's review how you can make use of access restriction policies of APIM to throttle the requests.

Access restriction policies in APIM

Access restriction policies regulate the way APIs are consumed by the subscribers. Different policy options are available, and you can read more about them here: `https://docs.microsoft.com/en-us/azure/api-management/api-management-access-restriction-policies`.

The most important access restriction policies that apply to the monetization situation are listed in the following table:

Policy	Description
Limit call rate by subscription	Restrict the number of requests to an API for a specified period, on a per-subscription basis.
Limit call rate by key	Restrict the number of requests to an API for a specified duration, on a per-key basis.
Set usage quota by subscription	Enforce a limit on the bandwidth quota or usage volume, on a per-subscription basis. These limits are renewable on a configurable time period basis.
Set usage quota by key	Enforce a limit on the bandwidth quota or usage volume, on a per-key basis. These limits are renewable on a configurable time period basis.

When it comes to request throttling, there are a few other additional options that are supported by APIM, such as IP address-based or user identity-based throttling. Depending on your specific scenario, you can use one or more policies to limit API usage spikes from a consumer.

In the next section, we will discuss how to generate consumption reports using APIM, which can then be fed to the billing engine to generate invoices.

Measuring API consumption

APIM provides usage reports that can be used to calculate the consumption of the respective APIs. The data in these reports is accessible through the REST API provided by the Azure Management SDKs.

You can find the complete list of usage reports available for APIM here: `https://docs.microsoft.com/en-us/rest/api/apimanagement/2019-12-01/reports`.

To calculate consumption, the following reports can be used:

- **List by Product**: List of usage data by product (reference: `https://docs.microsoft.com/en-us/rest/api/apimanagement/2019-12-01/reports/list-by-product`).

- **List by Subscription**: List of usage data by subscription (reference: `https://docs.microsoft.com/en-us/rest/api/apimanagement/2019-12-01/reports/list-by-subscription`).

Usage consumption statistics record schema

The reports provide an array of unique usage summary records, for a combination of product and `subscriptionId`, in the following format:

```
{
"name": "",
        "userId": "/users/1",
        "productId": "/products/5600b59475ff190048060002",
        "subscriptionId": "/
subscriptions/5600b59475ff190048070002",
        "callCountSuccess": 13,
        "callCountBlocked": 1,
        "callCountFailed": 0,
        "callCountOther": 0,
        "callCountTotal": 14,
        "bandwidth": 11019,
        "cacheHitCount": 0,
        "cacheMissCount": 0,
        "apiTimeAvg": 1015.7607923076923,
        "apiTimeMin": 330.3206,
        "apiTimeMax": 1819.2173,
        "serviceTimeAvg": 957.094776923077,
```

```
        "serviceTimeMin": 215.24,
        "serviceTimeMax": 1697.3612
}
```

A daily/weekly/monthly export job can be created to copy the consumption data to your billing and invoicing system in order to calculate the charges based on the pricing plans defined for the products.

You must pay careful attention to your billing calculation engine, as that could either make or break your productization strategy.

API analytics

APIM provides built-in analytics for the list of APIs published. This is useful for analyzing the performance and usage of the various APIs.

You can read more about it here: `https://docs.microsoft.com/en-us/azure/api-management/howto-use-analytics`.

You can extend the analytics capabilities by using the following options:

- Stream events to Azure Event Hub (reference: `https://docs.microsoft.com/en-us/azure/api-management/api-management-howto-log-event-hubs`).

- Log requests with Azure Application Insights (reference: `https://docs.microsoft.com/en-us/azure/api-management/api-management-howto-app-insights`).

It goes without saying that all strategies must be based on insights derived from data. API Analytics is perhaps the most important tool for business decision-makers. The usage analytics insights provide trends and patterns about the consumers. This is useful intelligence for planning the product roadmap, including any marketing strategies that are geared toward improving the consumption of your APIs.

Summary

In this chapter, you have learned how APIs can generate value for an enterprise through an intelligent monetization strategy. You have studied the key drivers behind monetization, and the various models that can be used as part of a productization strategy.

An example reference architecture was also studied to explain the important aspects involved in planning your productization strategy both from a business and technical perspective. You should be familiar now with applying the concepts presented in this chapter for your API publishing requirements in Azure.

You should also be comfortable with identifying and elaborating on the business capabilities that must be part of your backlog to implement an end-to-end productized API platform.

APIM is a robust product offering in Azure from Microsoft. You must plan to explore the technical capabilities it provides and start using them for your API-centric solutions in Azure.

In this book, you have studied the benefits of API-led architectures for a modern enterprise. You have also explored the capabilities of Azure that you can make use of to plan and deploy your APIs using a robust DevOps life cycle process. Additionally, you studied how effective monetization strategies can lead to value generation through your digital assets. If you are a business or IT decision-maker, you should be able to readily apply the concepts to define product roadmaps and set up a high-performance development team.

Further reading

- White paper on APIM driving the API economy: `https://azure.microsoft.com/en-in/resources/azure-api-management-driving-digital-transformation-in-todays-api-economy/`

- Top five API monetization models: `https://nordicapis.com/top-5-api-monetization-business-models/`

- API monetization models, strategies, and best practices: `https://blog.api.rakuten.net/api-monetization/`

- How to monetize your APIs using APIM: `https://azure.microsoft.com/en-us/blog/how-to-monetize-apis-with-azure-api-management/`

- Use APIM for API monetization: `https://github.com/Azure/api-management-monetization`

`Packt.com`

Subscribe to our online digital library for full access to over 7,000 books and videos, as well as industry leading tools to help you plan your personal development and advance your career. For more information, please visit our website.

Why subscribe?

- Spend less time learning and more time coding with practical eBooks and Videos from over 4,000 industry professionals

- Improve your learning with Skill Plans built especially for you

- Get a free eBook or video every month

- Fully searchable for easy access to vital information

- Copy and paste, print, and bookmark content

Did you know that Packt offers eBook versions of every book published, with PDF and ePub files available? You can upgrade to the eBook version at `packt.com` and as a print book customer, you are entitled to a discount on the eBook copy. Get in touch with us at `customercare@packtpub.com` for more details.

At `www.packt.com`, you can also read a collection of free technical articles, sign up for a range of free newsletters, and receive exclusive discounts and offers on Packt books and eBooks.

Other Books You May Enjoy

If you enjoyed this book, you may be interested in these other books by Packt:

Enterprise API Management

Luis Weir

ISBN: 978-1-78728-4-432

- Comprehensive, end-to-end guide to business-driven enterprise APIs
- Distills years of experience with API and microservice strategies
- Provides detailed guidance on implementing API-led architectures in any business

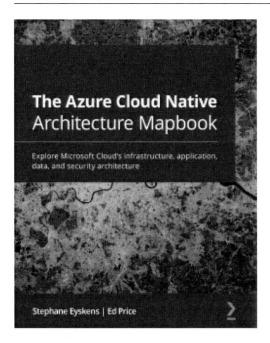

The Azure Cloud Native Architecture Mapbook

Stephane Eyskens, Ed Price

ISBN: 978-1-80056-2-325

- Discover the key drivers of successful Azure architecture
- Implement architecture maps as a compass to tackle any challenge
- Understand architecture maps in detail with the help of practical use cases

Packt is searching for authors like you

If you're interested in becoming an author for Packt, please visit authors. packtpub.com and apply today. We have worked with thousands of developers and tech professionals, just like you, to help them share their insight with the global tech community. You can make a general application, apply for a specific hot topic that we are recruiting an author for, or submit your own idea.

Share Your Thoughts

Now you've finished *Designing API-First Enterprise Architectures on Azure*, we'd love to hear your thoughts! Scan the QR code below to go straight to the Amazon review page for this book and share your feedback or leave a review on the site that you purchased it from.

https://packt.link/r/1801813914

Your review is important to us and the tech community and will help us make sure we're delivering excellent quality content.

Index

Made in United States
North Haven, CT
07 November 2021